WRESTLING WITH LIFE

STORIES OF MY LIFE
IMMERSED IN THE SPORT OF WRESTLING

Phil Nowick

authorHOUSE®

AuthorHouse™ LLC
1663 Liberty Drive
Bloomington, IN 47403
www.authorhouse.com
Phone: 1-800-839-8640

Published by AuthorHouse   02/25/2013

ISBN: 978-1-4567-5818-9 (e)
ISBN: 978-1-4567-5819-6 (hc)
ISBN: 978-1-4567-5820-2 (sc)

Library of Congress Control Number: 2011904889

CONTENTS

INTRODUCTION

I remember sitting in my hotel room in Tulsa, Oklahoma in Janurary, 2010. It was just before the finals of the Tulsa Nationals, perhaps the toughest and most prestigious kids wrestling tournament in the world. My phone lit up and it was just the person I wanted to talk to, my identical twin brother, Phil Nowick. Aglow in the accomplishment of our tiny wrestling club, I didn't know what to tell him first. We had two wrestlers in the finals and a half a dozen medalists. Moreover, heads were beginning to turn: A wrestling club from Colorado was now standing toe to toe with the clubs from the traditionally more powerful Midwestern and East Coast states. We belonged!

My brother's voice was solemn. He did not ask how I was or how our club fared in the tournament. Phil had been unable to make the trip to Tulsa because of an angry full body rash and what everyone assumed (or hoped) was a bad viral illness. "My cancer is back", Phil stated plainly. "I got a scan and it's in my liver this time. I don't have a rash. I'm jaundiced because the cancer's blocking my bile ducts. I guess you know what that means."

I *did* know what that meant. I am a physician. The numbers, statistics and survival rates of colon cancer had long ago been drilled into my head. Phil had been diagnosed with colon cancer in 2008. After surgery to remove the tumor, the initial rounds of chemotherapy had been promising. In 2009, Phil's scans and blood tests for tumor markers had been 100% negative for the better part of a year. It meant we needed a miracle.

I told no one. I went to the tournament that night and coached the finals. The team wrestled brilliantly. Two champions! Everything Phil had worked for, the love and energy he had poured into his young athletes had come to fruition.

That night I lay in bed, barely able to move under the gravity of what my brother had told me. We had an uphill battle ahead and a gruesome one at that. There would be no promises, but we would do what a lifetime in the monastic path of wrestling had taught us: keep fighting.

Somewhere between sleep and wakefulness a vision appeared to me. A figure somewhat reminiscent of the character "Q" from Star Trek, The Next Generation appeared. He quickly blurted "Dave, I like you so I wanted to come to tell you your brother is going to be all right." He paused wryly and said " . . . But it's not going to look like you think it will" Then Q smiled, almost laughing and disappeared.

The miracle we prayed for did come in the form of the book "Wrestling With Life". As Phil's physical form diminished, a wisdom and spiritual shine appeared. This lighthearted collection of stories could best be considered our memoires of growing up in the sport of wrestling. Phil's boundless enthusiasm and energy; his relentless pursuit of bliss; his commitment to live loudly as his most authentic self are all reflected in the stories he depicts. I can attest to one thing. These stories are true. I was there.

The first edition of the book included six short stories. Each chapter is priceless in itself, and the collection weaves a tapestry that encompasses Phil's humanity, his integrity and his ability to laugh at himself (and his ability to laugh at me). Not included in the first edition was "The Astros Incident," perhaps THE story of the Nowick twins. In memory of my brother and the close relationship we shared, I have recounted this tale for Phil and included it in the second edition. I hope you enjoy it as Phil certainly did.

The last words Phil writes in his book are: "Wrestling Brings the Light." Like most people would, I initially read this in the declarative, as a statement. However, over time I have realized that these four words are my brother's legacy to me. They are, in fact, an open ended question, much like a question on a final exam:

"Wrestling Brings the Light." Please defend or refute. Feel free to bring in personal experience, expert testimony, and factual evidence to support your answer.

My answer to Phil's question is coming in the soon to be released film "Wrestling With Life—The Documentary." One could consider this book the prequel to the film. The movie picks up where Phil's wonderful book leaves off. It's has a substantially different tone but probes deeper into the subject matter Phil introduces. I hope you will enjoy "Wrestling With Life", the book and the movie. I know I have enjoyed the journey through both and am thankful to share it with you.

Namaste,

Dave Nowick M.D.

STORY 1

ITEMS OF EVIDENCE

Destiny is not a matter of chance, it is a matter of choice;
it is not a thing to be waited for, it is a thing to be achieved.
— William Jennings Bryan

Let's go back to the beginning, start on a lighter note. I firmly believe
that the decision to participate in wrestling was a life-saving choice
for me and my twin brother, David. It presented a distinct fork in the
road through which we were able to channel our extreme abundance of
combative energy, our somewhat criminal intellects, and our burning
desire to find the answer to the question "What would happen if
we … ?".

Conversely, I have equal convictions that there currently exists a
parallel universe in which we did not link our paths to the great sport
of wrestling—it's not pretty. In this alternative reality, David and I share
a cell in a maximum-security prison, and we are currently plotting
an audacious escape. I can't say for sure what crime took us down,
ultimately—I'm no soothsayer. I can only present the following items of

evidence that preclude us from any other fate, absent a defining moment in which a discerning Little League baseball coach changed everything. I tremble when I imagine the consequences.

Item of Evidence #1: Kindergarten Chaos

What kind of kid gets expelled from school on the first day of kindergarten? What heinous act could lead to banishment prior to uttering your first letter of the alphabet? I can answer that question; so can my brother. What makes the accomplishment remarkable is the fact that we managed to achieve such a feat in less than three hours. Kindergarten at Greenwood Elementary in southeast suburban Denver consisted of half days: 8:00 a.m. to noon. The class was commanded by Mrs. Blue, a sweet, diminutive, ancient woman (she was at least seventy-five years old and stood no more than 4' 10") who had been teaching at the school since its inception.

David and I were somewhat secluded from other toddlers during our preschool years. Our mother, Susan—a living saint—took on the bold task of staying at home with us for the first five years of our lives before returning to work to run my father's medical practice. Compared to other mothers, Susan was not quite as concerned with the socialization of her twins up to that point. We had access to a best friend and coconspirator at all times, and we played together endlessly. We never lacked for fun and company. Sure, there had been some red flags in preschool, but who can really discern a pattern in behavior at that age? As with young jungle cats or tree gorillas, any activity with which we were saddled turned into play-fighting or, more accurately, fighting. Thus, our early childhood development resembled more *Lord of the Flies* than *Leave it to Beaver*. We had absolutely no sense of physical boundaries. It was perfectly okay for me to shove a pile of Play-Doh down David's throat, and I similarly didn't take offense when David would slap me in the chops in order to gain control of the last bite of a Milky Way bar.

Hence, upon entering our classroom full of happy, innocent toddlers, we took the place by storm that first day. Mrs. Blue made her first mistake sometime in the middle of the morning by lining the class up from tallest to shortest. We were placed in the back of the line—not a good way to appease a pair of five-year-old Napoleons. Our only academic assignment for that momentous day was to finger paint a crude picture with chocolate pudding as the medium and white construction paper as the canvas. One by one, we approached Mrs. Blue, who would then take a dollop of the dark-brown, sweet mix and place it gingerly upon the paper. Like obedient angels, each of the other children accepted his lot and commenced with his first ever act of scholarly imagination.

My brother reached his place in line in front of me. I was dead last and growing more surly by the second. Mrs. Blue broke eye contact with me—her second and fatal mistake—while preparing my brother's palette. I instantaneously seized the opportunity by scooping a giant heap of pudding from the bowl and taking a long, lustrous slurp from my hand. As was common practice, I wiped the remainder on my brother's face. He immediately retaliated, and a friendly brawl ensued. It didn't look friendly to Mrs. Blue—she was horrified. However, because she was so small and elderly, she did not have the physical capacities to separate us. The situation escalated, and my brother gained the upper hand by grabbing my hair and shoving my head into the pudding bowl. He then began intermittently letting me up for air, a practice that resembled kind of a crude, chocolaty form of the waterboarding that has become all the rage with CIA-types these days.

I laughed hysterically as pudding spewed out my nose, but Mrs. Blue was sure I was pleading for my life. She swatted us with her purse to no avail. She was forced to leave the room to find a janitor to end the fracas. At this point, with no authority present, other children left their tiny desks and approached us in hopes of also garnering a larger portion of the confection. Neither David nor I was in a generous mood, and we quickly resolved our dispute in favor of the larger goal: defending the pudding bowl at all costs. Like pudding-covered savages, we beat back every advance. Most of these kids had been raised on Dr. Spock, time-outs, and proper play dates, and they were experiencing—quite literally —life kicking them in the teeth for the first time. Once the surge of kindergartners became too great, we opted for the tactic of hurling the chocolate mess at approaching enemies.

Finally, the bedlam subsided when the aforementioned janitor lifted us up by the napes of our necks and carried us outside by our shirt collars. Mrs. Blue had instructed him to take us out back and, as if we were fresh inmates, hose us down. The custodian abided, and we were then placed on the flatbed of his truck to dry off in the hot sun. Minutes later, Susan arrived, somewhat mortified but not surprised. "Those are bad boys. Bad, bad boys," Mrs. Blue shrieked. "Don't you ever bring them back." At the end of the day, some sort of behind-the-scenes deal was cut, and we were allowed to return on probationary status. But the fun at Greenwood was just beginning.

Item of Evidence #2: School Play Mayhem

In our youth, my brother and I had dueling thespian careers that brutally collided in tryouts for Greenwood Elementary's fifth-grade production of *Robin Hood*. I was prone to pop culture roles, starring as young Michael in the third-grade production of *Peter Pan*. My brother opted for more classical roles, starring as Macduff in the fourth-grade production of Shakespeare's *Macbeth*. We could have coexisted, perhaps collaborated on a few projects as each of us expanded his reach. Instead, one unspeakably violent interlude ended it all. Sadly, I suppose there was simply not enough room for two creative supernovas in the same acting universe. How did it all go so wrong?

It is impossible to have identical twins each in starring roles in the same play. The audience simply won't buy it. Inevitably, one twin wins out and the other must disguise himself heavily and settle for a measly background role. Hence, the money was on the table at tryouts in 1978 for *Peter Pan*. Going into auditions, David and I had learned that our older sister, Kim, had secured the lead part of Wendy, virtually ensuring that one of us would be picked as baby brother Michael. My brother went first. Mrs. Bridges, our gigantic, androgynous, Texan music teacher sat stone-faced, judging as David read aloud. He started off strong but stuttered on a couple of words, and I knew the part was mine. I stepped up to the podium, turned on the theatrical charm, and owned that part. David was relegated the role of Lost Boy #4, a plebeian part with no speaking lines.

The role of Michael was a bit of a double-edged sword, however. I had no problem with the material—Peter Pan was an audience favorite, and significant buzz radiated among the theater-going parental community as opening night approached. My lines were a bit campy—you know, cute kid stuff—but everybody has to start somewhere. I didn't feel as if I was selling out. The costume, however, was a problem. Recall if you will that the children in the play (Wendy, John and Michael) are awoken from their slumber and wear pajamas during the duration of the play. Mrs. Bridges chose the color pink for my outfit and insisted that I tote a teddy bear throughout the entire production. Although the garb would certainly never be mistaken for macho, it was the required uniform. Anything for the show, I rationalized. If any masculinity lines were crossed, the gray area probably popped up when I learned I would be required to wear makeup. "The stage lights dim your features," Mrs. Bridges told me, and I squirmed as my sister applied a light coat of rouge and cherry lipstick to my face.

The tension started at dress rehearsal. My brother maintains, to this day, that I emerged from behind the curtain looking like an eight-year-old transvestite. I don't think it was that bad. But David and our collectively claimed best friend, John Burke (a lifelong friend who, at the time, was the only kid demented enough to play with us) snickered openly as I read my first line. "What's so dern funny?" Mrs. Bridges asked with authoritarian, Lone Star bravado. She was clearly annoyed at the disturbance. "Nothing," they each replied, giggling, and then the entire cast giggled in kind. I seethed as we made it through the conclusion of the rehearsal, and I planned appropriate countermeasures.

Showtime came, and the taunts continued from David and John. Similar scoffs had spread among some other male members of the cast. Unshaken, I shined through the first act in conjunction with my older sister—a highly acclaimed performance. As the second act began, I reckoned the hay was in the barn with regard to the critics, so I set my eyes on payback. I had put great thought into the matter since dress rehearsal. I knew my opening existed in the crucial battle scene in which Captain Hook and his pirates hold captive Pan and the Lost Boys, who are relying on the young pajama-clad heroes to free them. As the scene unfolded with spectacular sword fighting, I knew my brother's arms would be bound behind his back on the plank of the ship, leaving his abdomen wide open. With the audience focused on the action at hand, I slipped over to David and, with absolute stealth, administered the mother of all cheap shots—the liver punch. Any playground thug will tell you that proper delivery of the liver punch is more art than science. To ensure maximum pain and total debilitation, an upward angle is required along with an exacting delivery with the middle knuckle landing just below the ribs. I hit it right on the money, and my smug twin brother went down like a sack of potatoes, writhing in pain. The scene ended and the actors cleared the stage. A smattering of confused laughs emerged from the crowd. Lost Boy #4 lay prostrate on the stage floor, perhaps hamming it up after the battle scene. David and I knew better; as he staggered to his feet, we exchanged a glance that only twins can share, and with it, dual messages. Mine: "Don't mess with the kid in pink pajamas, pal." His: "It's a long life, young Michael. Watch your back."

Fast forward a year to the fourth-grade production of *Macbeth*. The play was headed by my brother's homeroom teacher, Mr. Lopes. Several noteworthy traits made him ideal for the twofold role of producer and director. Mr. Lopes was a stellar teacher in all subjects, owing to his creativity and enthusiasm. He hailed from New York and grew up on Broadway productions. In the process, Mr. Lopes had contracted an incurable case of the drama bug (a signed picture of Bob Fosse sat front and center on his desk), and it shined through in every aspect of his life. Given his Big Apple roots, Mr. Lopes was gutsy and, at times, combative. He suffered no fools in the classroom and in return was always willing to challenge the school administration on our behalf. Finally, Mr. Lopes was openly and fabulously gay at a time when that lifestyle was still incredibly taboo in education. He had handled any resistance to his lifestyle with an unapologetic grace. It was impossible not to like the guy.

I was compelled to settle for the pedestrian role of Donalbain for two spurious reasons. First, a scheduling error between my people and Lopes's people regarding a somewhat involved game of kickball resulted in my unintentional tardiness to tryouts. Second, I was unfairly typecast as a one-trick pony, based on my work in *Pan*. Mr. Lopes was looking for something darker. David had been buttering Mr. Lopes up for weeks in homeroom, math, and spelling; and he landed the important, brooding role of Macduff. The outcome was predetermined—I would be sitting the bench for this one.

This was David's time to shine, and as a result, the Nowick family immediately had a diva in our midst. Macduff demanded a hand-crafted sword made out of plywood to round out his costume. Our dad immediately got to work on the task. Macduff required his hair feathered and blow-dried in the mornings to impress the cast. Our sister was recruited for that job. Macduff stipulated that a Hostess Ding Dong, warmed in the microwave for exactly thirty seconds (so as to warm the confection but not disturb its consistency; try it—simply amazing) and placed on the family's prized *Six Million Dollar Man* plate, would be prepared by our mother every day at 7:30 p.m. on the dot while he read his lines. Postrehearsal, Macduff required exclusive access to our Atari video game system to unwind. He was absolutely insufferable.

The production was a smashing success. Mr. Lopes had the cast of eleven-year-olds reciting Shakespeare as if it were their native tongue. The set, music, and visual effects were over the top, and the critics gave five stars across the board. I rattled off my one measly line in ten seconds and immediately put my head on a swivel. My brother had a memory like an elephant's, and I was sure that retribution was coming. Surprisingly, the event went off without a trace of violence, and I considered the whole liver punch matter settled, water under the bridge. I couldn't have been more mistaken.

It all ended in the fifth-grade production of *Robin Hood*. Given our history, David and I would both be gunning for the lead role of the swashbuckling egalitarian Robin. Mrs. Bridges was back at the helm and threw a curveball to everyone at tryouts, which she held in the school gymnasium/cafeteria. She had chosen another fairy tale, but on the heels of *Macbeth*, she was determined to put a newer, grittier spin on the production. Thus, in lieu of simply reading lines with the auditioning hopefuls, she opted for improvisational acting exercises. Everything within reach—dodgeballs, tumbling mats, climbing ropes, etc.—became a theatrical prop, and she dictated various acting scenarios, putting the actors on the spot, seeing how they responded to pressure. I knew what Bridges was going for. She wanted to see the human side of Robin. I tried to conjure his most primitive motivations: the pain of the proletariat class, the hunger and frustration of the poor, the incorruptible desire to make things right. I brought with me an old actor's trick to keep my mind limber: a plastic baggie full of Cap'n Crunch. I let the munching sound clear my head as the scraping pain on the roof of my mouth sharpened my focus.

I was standing in line next to my brother when Mrs. Bridges ambled over in our general direction. She gawked for a moment at me and my brother, her hulking six-foot frame casting a shadow over us, seeming to engulf every bit of light beaming through the cafeteria windows. I sensed that we were on the brink of a nightmare scenario: David would be my improv acting partner. "Y'all two twins git up on that balance beam and act like y'all er crossin' a bridge. 'Cept there ain't near nuff room for ya to git by. Ya follow me?" she boomed.

I did follow. I would be carrying my hack of a twin through the exercise, and I prayed that he wouldn't screw it up. We both ascended the four-foot-high balance beam and took our positions. I took two tentative steps toward David and began to utter my first impromptu line in a sort of cockney British accent: "I say, good man, I see that we have met in the middle of this bridge. Would you be so kind as to … " And then I saw the look of malice in my brother eyes. I didn't have time to register anything else, but suffice it to say, the karma of the liver punch was coming home to roost. The force of a vicious clothesline blow that my brother sent special delivery to my face was sudden and bone-rattling. My feet flew in the air in front of me, and my descent to the gym floor was both comic and dreadful, arms and legs flailing in the air. I landed directly on my head and blacked out upon impact. I awoke to the earsplitting screech of an irate and sickened Mrs. Bridges. She bellowed an expression that David and I would hear time and time again until adulthood: "What in *the* hell is wrong with you boys! Git the hell out of here."

And so it ended. Neither of us ever acted again. My brother sacrificed both of our careers in favor of settling his vendetta, and he stood atop the beam in triumph, laughing hysterically. To this day, I think he regards it as one of his greatest moments. The boy in the pink pajamas went down, and he went down hard. All hail Macduff.

Item of Evidence #3: Caveman Wars, Chocodiles, and the Suicide Flip

The summer of 1980 was truly a season of transition in all respects. America was in the last year of the Carter administration, and we had begun to shrug off rampant inflation, an OPEC oil embargo, disco, and polyester. Our family ate dinner together at 6:00 p.m. sharp every day. Amid the occasional flying fork from our father, Martin, in retaliation for gross and wanton insubordination, we all clung to Walter Cronkite's nightly report on the status of the Iran hostage crisis. The 1980 presidential campaign was a close second in terms of headlines, and that Reagan guy seemed much cooler than Carter. My brother and I became huge fans—pure bandwagon hopping.

Although the aforementioned events did dominate the collective consciousness, a paradigm shift of far greater significance had taken place during that summer. The Hostess Chocodile (which was the next generation of Twinkie, elegantly dipped in chocolate) hit the West Coast. Denver, in my belief, was a test market, and thus the highly coveted after-school snack/dessert was stocked at scant few grocery stores in limited supply. A future economics major, I received my first lesson in the power of supply and demand from the Chocodile. Like Pacino's character Tony Montana in *Scarface*, David and I would leverage this magnificent treat to evolve from undersized, ten-year-old also-rans into serious power brokers in the yards and playgrounds of Greenwood Village. We would utilize this clout to overthrow the biggest tyrant our neighborhood had ever known—his name was Dooley.

It all started civilly enough. Sometime early in June our doorbell rang, and my mother answered the door. David and I followed and squinted through the bottle-glass windows in the front of our home, which made guests or solicitors appear freakish, like a living Salvador Dali painting. A man introduced himself; he was our new neighbor from across the yard. (Modern-day subdivisions are replete with high fences and postage-stamp backyards. Such boundaries did not exist in our neighborhood in 1980; yards flowed endlessly into other yards, creating endless fields of play. As a result, up to thirty neighborhood kids would gather each day and form an endless game-playing organism able to mutate from moment to moment to soccer, freeze tag, football, baseball, Slip 'n Slide—you name it. The youth I coach today in wrestling seem to be burdened with intense, Little League parental supervision, absolute competitive organization, and replica jerseys of professional teams as requisites to participate in sports. Conversely, during my childhood, if you were anything, you proved yourself in the yards. I see commercials on television today encouraging kids to put down the video games and play for at least thirty minutes per day. I have to laugh. Some of the biggest spankings my brother and I ever endured were the result of our playing far past dark in some remote yard blocks away).

The man introduced his sons, Tim (age thirteen) and Dooley (age fifteen). He was an oil executive, and they had just moved back from the Middle East—Saudi Arabia most recently, but also a stint in Iran. His sons had lived somewhat of a nomadic existence, he explained, traversing back and forth between Texas, Oklahoma, and the Middle East. Colorado has always been a redheaded stepchild of the US energy industry. The state has natural gas and oil, but it becomes feasible to drill through the mountainous soil only about once every twenty years, when gas prices reach crisis levels. Now they were the new kids, once again, in Denver. Their father had obviously been through this assimilation routine before, and he was finding allies for his sons as fast as possible. He had heard that our family had twins; perhaps we could show Tim and Dooley around, introduce them to other kids.

One of the sons, Tim, finally spoke up. "Can we jump on your trampoline?" he inquired. Anytime, my mom replied, no need to even ask permission, our yard was their yard. Susan was and continues to be an indefatigable caregiver. A nurse by training, her immediate instinct was to welcome and comfort outsiders or visitors—anything she could do to help. She would summon her two sons, and the friendship and trampoline-jumping would commence immediately.

We met in the backyard, and the look of disappointment on Tim's and Dooley's faces at our age and size was apparent upon first glance. "Aw. These kids are babies," Dooley whined. We literally had to stare up at both of them. My brother and I were barely four feet tall at the time. Tim seemed normal size, but Dooley was absolutely gargantuan. He towered to close to six feet tall and possessed a lanky frame with a certain dumpiness. His gut pooched slightly into open view under his AC/DC concert T-shirt. He wore thick glasses, the kind that automatically turned to sunglasses in the light—all the rage in the seventies. They hid his reptilian stare. His face displayed a healthy dose of acne that is common to fast-growing teenagers. "Shut your trap!" their father replied. "You damn well better be nice to these boys. Show them the ropes. Just have fun." He thanked us profusely, and his youngest son, Tim, acquiesced; he heard his father loud and clear.

Dooley, however, like many teenagers, found a way to contort the statement in his brain. The message that reached his cerebrum was the following: "Dooley. I want you to pick on these boys as much as possible. You are big for your age, and this might be the opportunity of a lifetime. Your brother, Tim, is growing older and now has the physical prowess to fight back. I want you to invent new ways to torment these kids—use your creativity. This will be excellent training for your career as a senior investment banker someday. I want these kids pushed to their absolute mental limit. Just have fun."

We began taking tentative turns on the trampoline, making nice until our parents disappeared into our house for coffee. My brother immediately started off on the wrong foot with Dooley. Staring inquisitively at his pimple-covered countenance, he asked naively, "How did you get so many mosquito bites on your face?" Tim exploded with laughter, and an instant bond was formed. David had innocently launched a barb that Tim would never dare hurl toward his much larger brother. (Although he dished out his share of punishment—he never had little brothers—Tim turned out to be a decent kid. He subtly looked after my brother and me and intervened cleverly if Dooley or other larger kids picked on us too much. He had a secret technique. If, for instance, Dooley had pinned us down and was trying to force us to eat a pile of dirt or dog poop, Tim would step in and pretend to finish off the deed. In truth, he would take it easy on us, allow us to expel the foul substance, and eventually let us go. Tim showed us our first *Playboy*, an issue with Suzanne Sommers—talk about starting with a bang—and taught us how to ride his skateboard. It was Tim who explained to us how the birds and the bees worked one night as we watched *Three's Company* on TV. We still didn't believe him; it sounded absolutely preposterous at the time).

Responding to Tim's laughs, Dooley took a malevolent step toward his brother but thought better of it and instead lunged forward like a leopard at David. That was yet another defining moment in our lives: David would be the first to receive Dooley's signature attack, which he called the brownie. You may know the brownie by another name: a wedgie, a snuggie—it's all the same. The basic concept involves your oppressor reaching down and hooking the top of your underwear from behind. He or she then yanks violently upward, causing the fabric of your undergarment to tear and disappear into your crotch, along with your dignity. No matter how erudite one's upbringing, we have all received a brownie at one time or another, and it hurts.

Dooley was an absolute mastermind when it came to brownies; through the duration of that summer we would receive hundreds and hundreds of them. Dooley conceived, at some point, a concept called "brownie time," in which he would grant David or me (or both of us) a five second head start and then easily chase us down with his lanky stride and dispense the agony. Like a mad scientist, he experimented with several variations of the brownie on the two of us: the "Tree Hanger," the "Over the Head," and a special adaptation called the

13

"Purple Herman," in which the brownie was delivered from the front, crushing the victim's young private parts. Dooley's crowning brownie achievement was the "Super Brownie." One night, midway through the summer, Dooley captured both of us on the trampoline and, as if he were an Olympic lifter performing the clean and press, simultaneously lifted us in the air, our collective legs kicking haplessly. Despite the pain and embarrassment, even we were impressed.

Given the above, "Why would David and I ever even leave the house?" you ask. It's hard to explain, but the rest of the summer rested on a tacit agreement. Tim and Dooley would allow us to hang out with them and do big kid stuff if we agreed to pay the penalty. Given our unnatural pain tolerance from countless wars with each other, it seemed like a square deal. Tim and Dooley were the cool kids in Greenwood Village. They had a bright, shiny newness, a mystique, because they had lived in so many exotic-sounding places and, given their father's predilection for moving at the drop of a hat for his career, were spoiled rotten. Like German tourists, Tim and Dooley were almost too American, as if their notion of pop culture was formed from abroad and therefore overdone. They wore rock concert T-shirts exclusively, from events they had actually been to: Van Halen, the Rolling Stones, David Bowie, Scorpions, Ozzy Osbourne, and Blue Öyster Cult. They always had cash for Slurpees, they owned—and could use—several killer skateboards adorned with more rock band stickers, and they popped endless wheelies on their expensive BMX bikes. David and I developed some street credit in the yards by our mere proximity to the brothers.

Furthermore, Tim and Dooley were the only kids in the neighborhood with cable TV, the ultimate luxury for TV-watching kids at the time. They were the first to discover MTV and ESPN, in an era when both networks resembled modern cable access shows. Most importantly, an odd truce evolved with Dooley around our only common interest: professional wrestling. Tim was lukewarm to the spectacle, and their father would protest at times in favor of watching more mainstream shows: *Face* the Nation or 60 Minutes on Sundays, The Love Boat or Fantasy Island on Saturdays, or The Bob Newhart Show on weekday nights. We were Dooley's excuse to control the family TV during wrestling. "You said be nice to the twins, right?" Dooley's father had no retort.

Precable, the Denver media market was a professional wrestling wasteland. Residents were stuck with AWA All-Star Wrestling, which aired on Sunday mornings. We attended Hebrew school during the school year at that time spot, and the VCR had not yet been invented. Naturally, this conflict sparked huge controversy within the family. "What's more important to you? Having a bar mitzvah and becoming a man in the community or watching All-Star Wrestling," our Dad asked. Our answer did not please Martin and was overruled in a fashion that could politely be called vigorous; I think a flying shoe was involved somewhere in the process.

Postcable was a completely different story. Two TV stations from faraway lands (watching them seemed like tuning into Al Jazeera in modern times, it was so foreign) aired better pro wrestling products and had a greater variety of scheduling. New York-based WOR offered Vince McMahon's WWF (now WWE)—a northeastern wrestling franchise that would grow into a billion dollar pay-per-view empire—in its early form. Atlanta-based WTBS, owned by Ted Turner, offered Georgia Championship Wrestling (which would later develop its own wrestling kingdom on Turner's channel TNT and would ultimately sell to WWE). We watched it all, though; we didn't discriminate. The AWA featured a middle-aged champion named Nick Bockwinkel, a classic cheating heel who was seemingly unbeatable no matter how big of a pounding he took. We were all intrigued by a young, green challenger: Hulk Hogan, a giant, surfer-looking grappler who would go on in later years to completely transform the industry hand in hand with Vince McMahon in WWE. Georgia Championship Wrestling boasted a tag team that was simply awesome: the Road Warriors. These guys were really the first of the modern vintage of pro wrestler—barbaric, face-painting, power-lifting, roid-raging, young bucks who looked like they could easily step on the front line for any NFL team. WWF highlighted Dooley's favorite, Fijian hero Jimmy "Superfly" Snuka, whose signature diving headbutt off the top rope remains one of the top finishing moves of all time.

After a period of time, Dooley decided that watching such events on the TV did not satisfy his bloodthirst. He needed a live bout, and he would act as promoter and announcer. On a nightly basis, David and I would be pitted against each other on the trampoline in what amounted to a juvenile dogfight. "No fake stuff either. Full contact," Dooley proclaimed (this was an era when the viewing audience believed, truly believed, that pro wrestling was real and, perhaps as a result of this belief, preferred blood to theatrics). Neighborhood kids began gathering and making side bets with Dooley. "What do we get if we win?" we asked. Dooley mulled over the question. "The winner doesn't get a brownie for twenty-four hours," he decided. Talk about a powerful incentive. We fought like prepubescent gladiators with every inch of our being.

The high point (or low, depending on how you view it) of the series of clashes was the summer finale, which Dooley aptly named "Cave Man Wars." We had just finished watching a highly contested NWA tag team championship match in which the Road Warriors took on "Mad Dog" Buzz Sawyer and his brother Brett in a "foreign object" match. All four contestants were allowed to bring a single weapon into the ring (a chair, a pair of brass knuckles, a steel-toed boot, etc.) with which to bludgeon their opponents. The Road Warriors, as usual, dominated, and the announcer, "Mean Gene" Okerland, declared "Man alive, you would have to go back to caveman days to witness such a spectacle." Hence the name was born—"Cave Man Wars."

It was a balmy Saturday night; the sun had just begun to fade behind the mountains. The crowd of neighborhood kids was twice as large as usual for the bout. Dooley instructed us to go inside our house and choose our weapons. My brother and I pored through our toy closet downstairs. I immediately seized upon my foreign object: a blue Wiffle ball bat with the original Batman logo. My brother, always the thinker, made a puzzling and unconventional choice: our Duncan glow in the dark yo-yo. Yo-yo historians will tell you that the dangling toy was originally used in the sixteenth century by East Asian hunters as a hunting tool and weapon. Chinese or Philippine hunters would hide in the trees and drop a grooved rock attached to string on their prey or enemy. I was not aware of the toy's capacities for matters of combat and felt sure the match would be a walkover. I was wrong—dead wrong.

As the match began, Dooley rang the bell, which he had fashioned out of one of their steel cooking bowls from home. I cocked my Wiffle ball bat as David crouched like a chimpanzee and swung the yo-yo malevolently above his head. My first blow was my last; I swung for the fences and my brother ducked and whisked his much smaller weapon with perfect skill and dexterity. His yo-yo wrapped around my bat like a tetherball, and he yanked it out of my hands. The bat went flying into the crowd, and I was immediately reduced to hand to hand, guerrilla status. The fight ended quickly as I absorbed blow after precision blow to the shins, knees, and head. I held out as long as I could but submitted after two minutes. The crowd went wild; my brother was hoisted on all of the big kids' shoulders and carried around the yard in utter glory. I received my brownie from Dooley for the defeat, adding insult to injury. (Incidentally, I received countless rematches in our basement on Friday nights during The Dukes of Hazard and never won a single bout. I tried every type of weapon as my brother held true to the yo-yo, but the result was the same. My brother was simply a ninja with that yo-yo).

The "Cave Man Wars" elevated our status in the neighborhood immediately from plebeians to Spartan warriors. But it was a development along the lines of Marie Antoinette's "let them eat cake" that would take us to unprecedented heights in the yards. My brother and I had cornered the market on Chocodiles, and kids would do anything, absolutely anything, for a Chocodile. Our lead on the local supply of the treat stemmed from our relatively new standing as latchkey kids. Our father was working 24-hour shifts as an OBGYN with no medical partners and two offices, and my mother, like many budding female professionals in the work force, was thrust into the juggling act of balancing family and a full-time career. She simply had to step in and help manage Martin's practice. Doctors, for all their talent, are notoriously short on organizational skills and business acumen, and my father was no exception.

My brother and I thought the arrangement was the best thing since sliced bread. Our general after-school regimen involved gluttonous feasts, knock-down, drag-out fights, infinite pranks, and the inevitable cover-up or spin control all before my parents returned home at 6:00 p.m. for dinner. But my mother worried endlessly, constantly asking if we were okay and apologizing that we were left alone. "How are you feeling?" she asked my brother one day with genuine love and concern. David seized on the opportunity; I caught the drift too. "I miss my mommy!" he yowled. "Yes, Mommy," I chimed in, "my heart hurts when you are gone." Susan's eyes moistened, and she beseeched, "Is there anything I can do to make you feel better?" We both contemplated the question with false gloom. "Chocodiles," we said in unison, and, from then on, we never had less than eight boxes of Chocodiles in the house. My mother would drive two townships over, fifteen minutes out of her way, to the only grocery store offering the treat and clean them out.

We incidentally had ample support in our Chocodile consumption from Martin. Like us, he is to this day somewhat of a dessert fanatic. He also adored Chocodiles, and they became a staple as Nowick family after dinner cuisine. The biggest fight I ever remember my parents having originated from my father's decision to give my mother a birthday Chocodile in lieu of a birthday cake. He had been working furiously and either simply forgot or ran out of time to purchase a proper cake. He stopped by Angel's bakery on the way home from work, but they were plum out of cake. Martin had scheduled a dinner date with my mother at 6:30 p.m. He would have to improvise. Upon returning from dinner, he asked my brother to adorn a Chocodile with candles and Hershey's Kisses. We lit the candles and sang "Happy Birthday," but my mom was not pleased. Birthdays are everything to her—she spared no effort to make everyone in our family feel special on that day and expected the same. Hostess products, in her view, did not cut the mustard. My dad caught hell that night and returned from work the next day with the most elaborate birthday cake I have ever seen.

David and I started using Chocodiles as currency for the simplest commodity: protection. We recruited our fourteen-year-old next-door neighbor, Danny Mooney, and bartered a price of one Chocodile per day if he would run interference with Dooley. Danny was no giant, but his entire family were hippies, and he had a way of negotiating peaceful resolutions. And, like magic, the brownies stopped. We then started offering Chocodiles in return for taking care of our outdoor household chores. As we grew older, our parents had increased our allowance for mowing our sprawling lawn, pulling weeds, cleaning the seventies-style rock garden, trimming bushes, etc. Based on the Chocodile payout, we were compensating these kids with slave labor wages. And we then had the idea of paying Danny's older sister, Sheila Mooney, to drive us to the King Soopers to obtain more Chocodiles, in addition to the normal family allotment, with our allowance. We accumulated the equivalent of Fort Knox in Chocodiles and hid the secret stash in the toy closet, next to the Wiffle ball bat and yo yo. We acted like the Federal Chocodile Reserve, controlling the supply of the baked delights based on our goals for the neighborhood economy. We commenced selling the Chocodiles for five times retail and plowed the money back into the business accordingly. Within weeks, we approached kingpin status.

Dooley's demise resulted from his own vanity. As the summer drew on, his grip over the neighborhood had slipped a bit. He was no longer the new guy—that luster had worn off, and many kids opted for strength in numbers, no longer fearing his physical intimidation as much. So Dooley took to taking extreme risks, like jumping his bike and skateboard, to impress the girls. During an afternoon trampoline session, "oohs" and "aahs" sounded from the peanut gallery of neighborhood kids after Tim's execution of a perfect suicide flip. (For trampoline neophytes, the key elements to a good suicide flip are bounding high in the air, nose-diving dangerously toward the trampoline, and turning a front flip at the last possible moment. It takes guts). Dooley sneered at his brother, obviously jealous. "That's nothing," he said. "I've done hundreds of suicide flips."

Tim challenged his brother, "If you think you're so hot, why ain't you done one?"

"Because it's too easy," Dooley replied.

It was then that my brother, a budding young genius, chimed in. "I'll bet Dooley could do a suicide flip off the balcony. Huh, Dooley?" he gushed in false admiration.

"Probably," Dooley mumbled uncomfortably; he sensed he was getting in over his head.

"No way," I added. "No one can do a suicide flip off the balcony. That's twenty feet up."

Tim piled on, "Come on, big man; let's see you do it if you're so tough."

Dooley's face flushed with anger, and we could sense he was about to extricate himself from the situation the way all bullies do, with violence. He took an angry step toward Tim, and I can still remember my brother's young voice stopping him dead in his tracks. "We'll give you an entire box of Chocodiles if you do a suicide flip off the balcony," David said.

Dooley stopped cold, looked at my brother, and licked his lips. "How many Chocodiles are in a box?" he asked greedily. "Twelve," I said. At the time, twelve Chocodiles had a neighborhood street value that couldn't be measured. They were rare and priceless commodities. Add to that the opportunity for Dooley to put himself in the books as the biggest daredevil ever in the yards. He couldn't help but take the bait.

We showed Dooley into the house, up the stairs, and onto our outdoor balcony that overlooked the Rockies. (Parents, for future reference, I would highly recommend a trampoline as a device for developing core strength, agility, and balance in kids, as well as a source of plain good old exercise and fun. But, never, I mean never, place the trampoline beneath a low roof or balcony. As you are about to read, the results can be dreadful). Dooley walked to the edge of the deck and stared ominously at the trampoline. It certainly looked higher when you were looking down. "Show me the Chocodiles," he demanded, trying to buy extra time. My brother and I complied and returned a minute later with the prize. By then Tim and other kids had started mocking Dooley. "Chicken! Bok, bok, bok. Chicken!" they yelled, and thus Dooley knew there was no turning back. He climbed up on the railing and squatted, a poor choice for a starting position if you ask me. He waited a full minute trying to gain his nerve, and the jeering intensified.

His dismount was a disaster, and he veered to the right side of the trampoline instead of dead center. We all began to realize that the magnitude of the jump, twenty feet onto a springy trampoline, was highly dangerous and stupid. In my mind's eye, it seemed as if it took an eternity for Dooley to descend, and he actually never attempted the flip. Given his miscalculation of the angle, he chose instead to abort the trick, trying to land on his feet to save his hide. He did, but his girth and velocity stretched the fabric of the trampoline all the way to the ground. Dooley was due for a second trip—this time upward—and it went even worse than his takeoff. The close proximity of his feet to the springs bounded him hopelessly high at a severe angle. Dooley's tubby frame tumbled sideways, resulting in his doing a kind of flying cartwheel through the air and onto our yard. He collided with the grass and dandelions with a sickening thud and then landed awkwardly on his shoulder, breaking his clavicle. He screamed in pain and wailed like a newborn baby in front of all the other kids, which marked the end of his rule of the yards.

We never saw Dooley again. Tim came around sporadically as summer turned to fall, and by the time school started, they had moved back to the Middle East, Yemen this time. My parents eventually found the Chocodile stash and severely curtailed our deal out of fear of childhood obesity. We would go on to hold our own in the yards during the next few years, but we never returned to the emperor status we had achieved in those delicious few weeks.

I could go on and on with other stories. I could tell you about the time in first grade when we were declared retarded by Greenwood school officials as a result of record low scores on aptitude tests. (They made the mistake of declaring recess as soon as you were done, so we opted to mark every answer *A* and finished in ten minutes). A month later, we tested at a fifth-grade reading level as we retook the test under my mom's angry supervision. I could tell you about the time we wrecked our babysitter's car when my brother and I decided to sneak into the vehicle and play *Speed Racer* by messing with the gearshift at the top of her steep driveway. The VW Bug rolled haplessly down the driveway and mangled a pine tree as we leapt from the vehicle. I could tell you about the time in which my brother, John Burke, and I crafted a water balloon shooter with twenty-foot range out of a Cool Whip container and surgical tubing and almost killed the boy next door.

But you catch the drift. With mentors like Tim and Dooley and our own predilections toward mischief, we were headed for trouble. Without some serious focus and discipline as we migrated toward high school and the bell curve of teenage growth kicked in, we were bound to be jettisoned from the football, baseball and soccer teams. Competition for spots on varsity teams was intense at our high school, and our miniature size, squatty frames, and plodding strides made us nonstarters. Nay, without a major change in direction we would have eventually found something else to get into besides sports—something bad—and we would have done so with unprecedented gusto. Consequently, I maintain a firm belief in our alternative reality as master criminals had we not found wrestling.

Salvation

The flyer came every fall and was distributed to all boys at Greenwood Elementary. "Cherry Creek Little Brothers Wrestling Team" the flyer read at the top. The rest of the flyer depicted the virtues of the sport and details of team practices, fees, etc. We would bring the red piece of paper home each year and beg our parents on our knees to to let us join the sport. Nothing doing, Martin and Susan said. They had both attended one and only one amateur wrestling match in their lives, during their days at East High School in Denver. A boy ended up breaking his neck and was taken away in an ambulance, they said. Stick to soccer, baseball and gymnastics. My mom also had more gentile aspirations for us. She had dragged us kicking and screaming to artsy endeavors such as school choir, piano and saxophone lessons with increasing frequency as we grew older, as if she were trying to stem the tide in our lack of civility. We joined the local reading and math clubs with equal protest. "You have to let us wrestle!" we carped. "Besides, we are virtually experts. We have been watching *All-Star Wrestling* for years! That kid was probably a wimp that got hurt. We know what we are doing." "It's not the same," my dad replied. "Different rules." Hence our requests were denied four years in a row—first through fourth grade. But we kept the dream alive.

Our gateway to wrestling actually opened at a Little League baseball practice. Our Coach, Steve Kakos, was an intense motivator and a stern but affable teacher. Our summer baseball team, the Guthrie Construction Rangers, had achieved strong success that year as we entered the fifth grade. David and I were able players and reached base quite often on walks because our strike zone was so scant, but we were no superstars. We played in the outfield. Conversely, Steve's son, Kevin Kakos, was a phenomenal athlete. In addition to serving as our pitching ace, Kevin was a championship wrestler in his age group. We were all shagging flies in the outfield to close out another long summer practice, and our attention started to waver. Kevin began roughhousing a bit with the other kids, and one of them remarked, "Don't mess with him. He can wrestle."

We were immediately fascinated, and out of the blue, my brother exclaimed to Kevin, "I know wrestling too. Let's see what you've got." The rest of the team marveled at David's courage. Kevin was modest and quiet, but he obliged the challenge—he couldn't back down to this half-pint and remain in good standing. The two dropped their gloves, and as the wrestling began, dust kicked up from the all-dirt field. Pretty soon I jumped in as well. Kevin got the better of us on technique and size, but we held our own. Mr. Kakos, who had been working with the pitchers, finally took notice. Ever the disciplinarian, he sprinted to the outfield and yelled, "Hey!" We sensed we were about to get a tongue-lashing for screwing around during outfield practice. Instead he yelled, "You two boys have to wrestle. You're pretty good." And so the fork in the road appeared, just like that. Our lives would be changed forever.

We attended our first wrestling practice in the fall under subterfuge. Mr. Kakos, a former high school wrestler and huge enthusiast, called on the phone and asked if we would be interested in trying the sport. Absolutely, we said. We had already received permission from our parents (a bold-faced lie), no need to talk to them. Our house was on the way, he would pick us up, he said. My brother and I were incredibly skilled at half-truths by that age, and we simply asked our parents if we could go to practice with Mr. Kakos on Monday. (Martin and Susan assumed we meant baseball, even though we were way out of season. By the time we returned, the jig was up and our parents finally caved. "You want to break your neck," Martin said, "fine with me. It's your life.")

We entered the red-matted wrestling room at Cherry Creek High School, and one thing struck us as odd. "Where is the ring?" I asked. Mr. Kakos replied that amateur wrestlers did not compete in a ring with turnbuckles and rope, but on mats. Odd, we thought. We actually ended up arriving at practice an hour late. Mr. Kakos had mistaken the time, so the teaching part of the practice was over. Thirty or so young boys engaged in "live" wrestling —actual combat—in front of us.

The youth coach, Bill Hendershot, who would become an irreplaceable mentor in our lives, greeted Mr. Kakos and directed Kevin over to some of the more experienced boys. Mr. Hendershot then looked at us and asked, "You boys ever wrestled (he pronounced it *rassled*) before?" Absolutely, we replied. He didn't buy it. "Okay then, let's get you going. Why don't we have you wrestle each other for awhile and you can show me some of your moves." No problem, we said. He blew the whistle and I immediately drop-kicked my brother in the chest. He countered with a forearm smash and leg drop a la Hulk Hogan. I responded with Jimmy Snuka's version of the victory roll. As usual, the bout degraded into my brother and me rolling around like rabid dogs. "Whoa! Whoa! Let's break this up here!" a gravelly voice thundered from across the room. It was Steve Foster, our future high school coach, who would become almost a father figure to us. He had poked his head in to see what up-and-coming youth had materialized. My brother and I were separated, huffing and puffing, and happier than we had ever been in our lives. Coach Foster winked at Coach Hendershot. "We need to teach these boys some wrestling. Holy cow, I thought they were going to kill each other, but it looks like we have a couple of winners. "

"Damn straight," Coach Hendershot replied. And that's what they did, taught us. We would grow, as you will read, to become highly successful wrestlers for our high school, and, more importantly, better people. Our alternative path of becoming high stakes gangsters would be diverted. We had found our calling.

Philosopher and shaman Alberto Villoldo once wrote, "Many people are subject to fate, but very few people have a destiny." As William Jennings Bryan wrote, in the quote above, we can either choose to let the circumstances of life and our own limitations steer us by chance, or we can take the wheel by making good choices. No matter one's age or experience in life, it's often difficult for all of us to know what that means from moment to moment. No one is born with the intention of life taking a left turn on him, like Dooley's suicide flip. We all need help, and as I've said, I strongly believe that some sort of communal and productive pursuit that brings joy is essential in finding this right path. Forks in the road form spider webs in front of us each and every day. I feel lucky and humbled that wrestling led us in the right direction, saving our lives that first time. It wouldn't be the last.

STORY 2

THE "KID"

*Do not allow the PRESSURES of competition
to be greater than the PLEASURES of competition.*
— Nick Purler

I want to tell you about the greatest age group wrestler in Colorado history. I will not reveal his name. Instead, for now, let's call him the "Kid". I only saw the Kid wrestle once. We were both twelve years old at the time, but apparently by that time he had reached rarified air in the world of age group wrestling. The Kid hailed from northern Colorado, the heart of wrestling country. He had begun his auspicious start in the sport at age four and, according to my coach at the time, Bill Hendershot (a fantastic age group wrestling coach for reasons you will glean later), had lost only a handful of matches in all those years. The Kid had won every Colorado state championship that he had ever attended. His state titles did not discriminate between Folkstyle (the traditional American style of wrestling), freestyle, or Greco-Roman (the two Olympic wrestling styles). In addition, Kid had won several national-level tournaments outside our state. I know this because the Kid literally wore his achievements on his sleeve. Like a twelve-year-old, eighty-pound, Russian commandant, he adorned himself in a trench coat-like garment that literally bore every medal he had ever won. This choice of wardrobe also gives you a glimpse into the Kid's demeanor—he was the best there was, he knew it, and he would not hesitate at the chance to inform anyone within shouting distance of this absolute fact, regardless of whether the topic interested the listener. Long story short: humility was not his strong point.

The Kid's dad— we'll call him Hank for now—was also legendary. Hank was the head of the first and largest real elite-level kids wrestling club in Colorado: the dreaded Hawks. In an era (1982) when the fashion merchandising of sports apparel had not yet taken off, the Hawks marched around in blue and gold sweat suits, color-coordinated "Dan Gable Special" wrestling shoes, and wrestling singlets made from a new space-age material we have come to know as spandex. The Hawks won the team title at every tournament by virtue of entering what seemed like a small army of wrestlers in every age division. Hank—according to Hank—was the Vince Lombardi of Colorado kids wrestling, and no team, future or present, would stand in the way of the Hawks' eternal dominance. Hank was also the worst Little League parent I have ever seen in almost twenty years of participation and coaching in wrestling and other sports. Hank was abnormally proud of his club, but he displayed a religious-like fervor when it came to the Kid's wrestling. Hank would openly taunt the Kid's opponents, their coaches, moms, dads, grandparents, and friends, before, during, and after matches. Referees dreaded Hank equally, as it was not uncommon for him to saunter out in the middle of the mat to interrupt a six or eight-year-old bout to bellow his displeasure with an official's call. Approximately every five minutes, Hank would restate his opinion that the Kid—his son, whom he molded from the cradle into a wrestling machine—would someday don Olympic gold. You get the picture—like father like son.

Like I said, I only saw the Kid wrestle once. I had a front row seat ... I wrestled him. Before we go into competitive specifics, let me paint the setting. We met in Pueblo, Colorado, at the state freestyle wrestling championships, which, in many ways, was as close to Darwin as I have ever been. Pueblo is a historic steel town in the Southern part of the state and also a wrestling hotbed. The town oozes toughness, and suffice it to say, it was not built on its amenities. The annual tournament was the Super Bowl of Colorado freestyle wrestling. The event was held at the local university in a gym that was far too small to accommodate the thousands of participants, who ranged all the way from six years old to college age. Bracket sizes in excess of seventy competitors were not uncommon, and the tournament lasted in duration from 8:00 a.m. until well past midnight for the finals. From a climate and topography perspective, Pueblo is more New Mexico or Arizona than Colorado. The temperature In July was above one hundred degrees, and the gym felt like a sauna. The noise level was deafening, a cacophonous mix of rabid parents and coaches and the constant drone of the loudspeaker calling an endless procession of wrestling matches. Good times.

I remember being in a particularly foul mood because of the surrounding conditions and for two additional reasons. First, one or more of my first four opponents had not showered in days, and my local teammates refused to sit next to me in the comically crowded bleachers because I smelled "like poo." Second, my twin brother, David, in an act of naked, unabashed gluttony, had both guzzled every drop of our 32-ounce bottle of Sunny Delight and devoured all three of the bagel and cream cheese sandwiches that our mother had packed for us. Given our Jewish heritage, bagels and cream cheese were like lifeblood for such events, and my brother had done the unthinkable. I was livid.

I also had a built-in advantage that day that I could never duplicate. My brother David and I were relative neophytes to the arena of big-time kids wrestling. We existed in a state of complete oblivion, paying our dues at our local club, having wrestled only in metro league events for almost three years. Unlike the Kid, my award inventory consisted of a couple of blue ribbons and a bevy of "certificates of participation." We would occasionally ask Coach Hendershot if we could attend some of the state and national-level tournaments with the more experienced wrestlers. For quite a while he would smile and reply, "You just wrestle. I'll let you know when you're ready." He confided in my parents that he did see something special in our ability, but every wrestler was different. His gut feeling was that we needed seasoning before being thrown to the wolves. That was good enough for us. The upshot of our inexperience was that we had no idea what to expect. We weren't involved in the "scene"; no one had ever seen us wrestle outside of the Denver suburbs. We were also clueless as to a) how good we were and b) more importantly, how good the other kids were—and our coach wasn't about to let us in on the joke. Coach Hendershot didn't believe a wrestler's reputation predicted the outcome of a match. He believed wrestling showed the winner.

Sometime in the midafternoon I met the Kid. Fresh off a shouting match with my brother over the whole SunnyD/bagel situation, I was steaming in seclusion, having been shunned by my teammates for both my demeanor and odor. The Kid sauntered over to me, sat right down next to me, and proclaimed, "This tournament is so easy. I can't even believe I'm here." I didn't respond; I wasn't sure if he was talking to me or himself. The Kid then examined my attire. I was adorned in polyester shorts, my torn "Cherry Creek Little Brothers Wresting" T-shirt, and the coup de grâce of beginner wrestlers: tennis shoes (Keds to be exact). If you know anything about wrestling, everybody wants to wrestle the kid in tennis shoes the first round—he stinks. "Don't you have wrestling shoes?" the Kid asked derisively. "No" I answered. My parents were practical about the matter: why buy the twins wrestling shoes until they prove they will stick with the sport? "Ah man," he replied, "I've got an easy one next round." Call it naivety, poor listening skills, ADD— whatever you want—I still didn't understand. The kid was talking about me. I was his next match, and he was sitting next to me blabbering, trying to insult and intimidate me. Thoroughly annoyed but still not completely informed, I finally cut him off and said, "Listen kid (no pun intended), I'm trying to get ready for my next match too, and if you don't leave me alone I'm going to beat the crap out of you. How does that sound?" The Kid looked at me quizzically and walked away, medals jingling.

I wish I could have bottled that moment and rode it the rest of my career. To me, the famous Kid wasn't the Kid. He was nobody; just an arrogant little bugger that talked to strangers and that I wanted to pummel. Nobody (not my parents, who could barely follow the rules of this barbaric sport at the time, my coach, nobody) had brainwashed me with the fact that I was nowhere in his league as a wrestler. My brother, who partially witnessed the conversation and was equally clueless, exclaimed, "If you wrestle that idiot, you better torture him." And I intended to.

Sure enough, the loudspeaker called my name to the assigned mat, and across from me stood the Kid, Hank giving him some sort of pre-match rubdown in his corner. Coach Hendershot offered me one brief but brilliant piece of advice. "Phillip," he said (he always called his wrestlers by their full names — another subtle way of making them feel important), "this guy is a shooter. Stay off him, and if he shoots, I want you to squeeze his lights out and hit that gator roll. I've seen you hit that move in practice on Christopher (his son), and it will work." Good enough for me.

Just as my Coach predicted, the Kid began the match in a catlike crouch and bounced around like Muhammad Ali, apparently showing off in front of the kid in tennis shoes. His first attack to my legs was lazy and from at least four feet away. I did as instructed; I stepped back, sprawled, and squeezed his head and arm until I heard an audible cry from the Kid. Bam! Bam! Bam!—three gator rolls. Six points on the scoreboard.

The Kid was stunned, and Hank exploded to the middle of the mat. "That was a choke," he howled, and a three minute delay ensued as he demanded the points be taken off the board and I be penalized or, even better, disqualified. The referee refused, and the match continued. They say "styles make fights," and the rest of the match was more of the same. The Kid kept shooting, and I kept squeezing. Hank kept screaming. Toward the end, because I knew only a few paltry wrestling moves, I sneaked in a handful of my patented cheap shots normally reserved for my brother in our basement. When the hand-wound clock struck zero, the gym went crazy. The mighty Kid had fallen. The Kid cried like Willem Dafoe in the movie *Platoon*, wailing on his knees, looking to the heavens like his life had literally ended. Hank walked up to me and shoved a meaty finger in my chest. "This ain't over; I'm protesting," he said. My coach intervened. People started crowding around me like I had won the Olympics, slapping me on the back and congratulating me. My coach was beaming. Apparently the Kid had beaten many of our top-level wrestlers time and time again, and he had finally dropped one.

The match was special to me—my first big win. It gave me a confidence I cannot describe, and I used that momentum to win a couple of national-level tournaments during the next year and many matches in the ensuing ten years.

"What happened to the Kid?" you ask. He never wrestled again. My teenage vanity led me to believe that the great Phil Nowick had scared him out of the sport. A few years later, I learned that Hank, as was his standard practice, had beaten the Kid somewhat severely that night to "straighten him out." The Kid blew a fuse and became a highly troubled youth. His hair grew down to his knees, and he became heavily involved in drugs. True story.

There are several morals to this tale. First, as a wrestling coach or parent, don't be Hank. Don't be anything like Hank. Be the exact opposite of Hank. Teach your kids to have fun at all costs. Constantly guard against the mentality, as parent/coach or both, of somehow measuring your kid's career and pinning your own happiness to it. Hank is living proof that if you don't enjoy the journey together, the trophies and titles mean absolutely nothing. Nothing rings truer about the sport than Nick Purler's quote at the beginning of this story: "Don't let the pressures of competition outweigh the pleasures of competition." If you are having a particularly bad day, substitute the word "competition" with the word "life," and you will find you have just given yourself some of the sagest advice you will ever receive.

Wrestling is, in my opinion, the most difficult sport to apply to this axiom. The training is excruciating. The wins are primal. The losses ... well, to be candid, wrestling is not a real fight, but you get more than your fill of simulated butt-kickings. The irony of the sport is that relaxing and focusing on having fun, even in the pressure cooker of national competition, will maximize your results.

Second, as a wrestler, don't ever let another human being tell you how good you are ... at anything. You decide that. Anytime a coach, parent, teammate, opponent, boss— whoever—tries to slot you into the pecking order of life before you have actually had a chance to perform, ignore them, smile at them, and thank them for the input. Then politely ask them to jump in a lake. Don't buy into rankings, brackets, gossip, etc. Just wrestle, just live, just have fun. I've had the honor of meeting some of the world's finest wrestlers—Arsen Fadzaev, Sergei Beloglazov, John Smith, Dave Schultz—but I've never met an undefeated wrestler. This means everybody is beatable. If you can't shake that mentality, buy a pair of vintage seventies Keds and wrestle in those for awhile—see how that works for you.

Namaste.

STORY 3

THE ASTROS INCIDENT: THE LOST STORY

Prelude

The following is truly the lost story from Phil Nowick's original book, "Wrestling With Life." Phil had, in fact, outlined this story and was prepared to insert it in the 1st edition. After a lifetime of recanting the debacle that follows to whomever would listen, Phil experienced a sudden bout of humanity. He left "The Astros Incident" out of the book.

So precious is this story (to him); so woven is this spectacle into the fabric of our existence as identical twins that I have decided to recant it for Phil. Please forgive any bias on my part. You will notice a certain similarity in my writing style to his for two reasons: 1. Like the other stories, this tale is true. 2. Also like the other stories we lived it together.

Dave Nowick M.D.

The Speedo.

"The suit of choice of elite swimmers around the world".

. . . And the required uniform for the Paradise Valley swim team in 1981. I'm told it improves aerodynamics in the water, but we will return to what the Speedo can and cannot do later.

What I need to discuss right now is the essence of being an identical twin. Have you ever heard someone say, "If there were just two of me . . . ." What if there **WERE** two of you? What if you were born with a built in best friend, partner in crime, extra set of hands, and support section. What couldn't you accomplish?

When you are an identical twin you do EVERYTHING with your brother: You eat together, you sleep together, you go to school together, you play sports together. You have the same birthday party (You get the exact same birthday presents). You get the same haircuts. You wear the same clothes (even if your parents do color code them so they can tell you apart). For all intents and purposes, the world sees you and your brother as one person.

So how do you distinguish yourself? Well, that's a complicated issue:

Twin law plainly states that in all endeavors – school, sports, work and family you root for your brother. You truly are his biggest fan. It's not a win unless you both win. It just feels wrong. So, outshining your brother (who has exactly the same physical gifts as you) is not only unlikely, but unnatural.

However, there *is a* way to gain an edge as a twin. One currency that matters. And it's the only currency that matters. It's called "the Juice." Here's how its works:

1. If you can publicly prove your brother wrong on matters trivial, that's small change. Maybe pennies.
2. If your brother purposely *does* something stupid that can be documented or re-enacted—Say a bad pose in a yearbook

picture or an unflattering role in a school play. That's good capital. Maybe dollars.

3. But if by chance, the twin God's should smile on you and something embarrassing should *happen to him*: an epically bad haircut (or man perm), an excessive and untimely weight gain (with or without the beret), having to have surgery on parts of the body we don't talk about. Now we are talking serious Juice. The sky is the limit. The bigger the incident the more it's worth.

4. 4. Once the Juice is in the bank, it can't be taken away. It's yours. You can bring it out whenever you want and usage is unlimited.

That brings us back to the Speedo. It was August 1981. I began this hot summer day by blow-drying my hair, "feathering it," and parting it down the middle. Mind you it was the 80's but we were barely over Disco. Phil and I were still much more Starsky and Hutch than Crockett and Tubbs. Miami Vice would come later.

Phil and I decided to go swimming with our friends. Paradise Valley (the country club where the Jews went to swim) was too far North for most of our friends. So Phil and I accompanied four teammates from the Astros (our little league baseball team) to Holly Pool, a public pool to the South. I had quit the swim team at Paradise Valley two years earlier. However, I wore my now undersized green and blue Speedo anyway because I thought it was macho.

The Astros had a game that night against the Phillies for the Cherokee League Division Title. The field was near to Holly Pool and the plan was to ride our bikes directly to the game.

The day droned on. The sun was hot. The girls were cute. The splash fights and fake WWF wrestling matches in the pool were epic. I got hungry and went to the snack bar. I confidently ordered a burrito when one of my friends warned me, "Don't do it. They are gross. No one eats them." I ignored him and ate it anyway.

Before we knew it we looked up and it was 4:41pm. The game was at 5:00pm. We were late and it was time to hurry. I threw my uniform over my Speedo and rode like heck.

We arrived at Honeywell field at 4:52pm. Phil and I weren't good at baseball. We probably wouldn't even play in the game, but the coaches were nonetheless mad. I was ordered to go to center field and catch fly balls to warm up. No batting practice for me.

It was running after fly ball #2 that I had one of those moments with my gastrointestinal tract: the moment where your bowels make a noise like a struggling steam boiler in the basement of an old refinery. I actually took a knee to get over the initial wave of pressure from the cannon ball that dropped into my lower abdomen. It was at that time I knew I was going to have *"issues."*

How to deal with these *"issues"* had everything to do with being an identical twin and nothing to do with normal human behavior. I had to manage risk. How much Juice was I willing to give up?

The only available restroom was a Sano-Let portable toilet. There was one such green monolith for the whole complex and everyone knew where it was. No one wants to use the Sano-let, but I had bigger reasons for avoiding it. The re-enactment of my session on the "porto-pottie" would provide my brother (and hence my teammates) with Juice for the rest of the season.

The game started and I went to sit on the end of the bench. I resolved to NOT use the Sano-let. To hold it no matter what. I could make it. I could stick it out. I wasn't going to play anyway.

BOOM!! In the bottom of the first inning, the boiler fired up again and the immense pressure that had been building inside me quadrupled. Mutiny had been struck in the galley of my bowels and *it was go time*. I needed to head to the Sano-let. Fast.

Dammit! What a lot of Juice to concede. I snuck away. My brother was in the field playing second base. Was there possibly a chance he wouldn't notice? Could I get off easy just this once? *No such luck!* As I circled behind the backstop my brother tracked me out of the corner of his eye. That knowing smile was there. He was already picturing the dramatization of the Sano-let.

As I passed the opposing dugout the situation got dire. The boiler went into overdrive, spasmodically blasting hot waves of strain, bludgeoning the walls of my intestines. I could feel fatigue begin to set in. My sphincter was hanging off the edge of a cliff, grip slowly loosening.

I needed to run if I was going to make it. I had about 50 yards to go, just beyond the right field fence. Looking back. I can't believe I even hesitated for a second to debate this. *But, for the love of God! The Juice I would hand over!* I could only picture my brother's musical depiction of Rocky (he often cast me in Sylvester Stallone roles while humiliating me) running to the Sano-let. So I ran: Part jog. Part waddle. Part speed race walk designed to move as fast as possible without agitating the explosive contents hammering away at my insides.

I would have made it. I truly would have. I had the reserve left. My mind was focused. There was no panic in my heart. The voices in my head were steadfast. "You WILL make it. Don't quit. Be tough. Right now, Dave, suck it up and do this right now!"

Then, first of two inexplicable strokes of bad luck came to be. Into my view came a large red mass, pulling me in like Jupiter exerting gravitational force on one of its tiny moons. An *enormous* woman in a red Mu-Mu stepped directly into my path. I hit her straight on.

"Oh I'm sorry young man. Are you all right? "

This was no time for niceties. The Sano-Let was directly behind her, maybe fifteen feet away. I stepped to the right but could not evade her large paws.

"Did I hurt you? Where are you going? The game is that way"

I broke the Mu-Mu woman's grip. I turned my back to her, backtracking from whence I came. I jump-cut hard to the left and circled wide around my adversary.

My college wrestling coach always preached that quitting happens in stages. No one breaks all at once. He cautioned to resist the first stages of quitting the most. The later stages were too easy, too comfortable. Unfortunately I would not meet my college coach for seven more years. And so when the voices in my head changed tone, I let my attention drift. Slowly at first the voices called like sirens calling unknowing sailors toward the rocks.

"Just let a little bit out, Dave. Relieve the pressure"

The last jump-cut had jolted my insides. I could feel the cracks in the dam start to widen. Maybe six feet left to travel. And then the soothing voices said something that made sense:

"Dave, You're wearing a Speedo.
It's too small. It will contain the diarrhea.
Just let a little bit out.
You're safe, Dave. You can always get rid of the Speedo. You
don't need underwear to play baseball.
Just take the edge off. Go ahead."

It seemed so harmless. Such a perfect coupe! My brother would never know. Yes!! I was meant to be on the Paradise Valley swim team. I was meant to wear a Speedo that day. A Speedo to protect me. A Speedo to shield me. A Speedo to be my savior. And so, still moving toward the Sanolet, maybe four feet away, I eased off the brakes, fully intending to slam them back on after just a millisecond.

There are two facts and only two facts that I am absolutely certain of in this Universe:

1. Where explosive diarrhea is concerned, once the flood gates open they cannot be shut. Period.
2. The Speedo, while tight and absorbent, is not designed to be used as any sort of barrier. In fact, if you look on the product insert it actually reads "Speedo is not effective as a device to contain explosive diarrhea or liquid feces of any type. Please exercise caution when wearing under bleached white baseball pants."

Like a muddy South American river, the burrito tinged waters raged out of my body. Immediately, the Speedo was overwhelmed and leaking like a sieve from all directions: waistline, pant-line, front, back. All decks spewed rust red lava. And then . . . . darkness

I was in the Sanolet. Dimly lit by a crack of the setting sun. The pressure was gone. Completely void. I felt the impulse to pull my pants down and sit on the toilet seat but there was no use. It was over. In my estimation over a liter of visceral foulness had been expelled in one giant peristaltic blast. Like the post-nuclear aftermath of Hiroshima and Nagasaki I stood calmly in awe of diarrheal devastation that previously had never existed on Earth.

I needed to assess the damage. Calmly and methodically I locked the door, took off my cleats, my socks and knee high baseball socks. I took off my previously white baseball pants. The news wasn't good. I forgot to take my baseball cap off as I removed my shirt. Thus, my only unsoiled article of clothing fell on top of my baseball pants, staining the brim. Finally, I took off the Speedo.

I am 11 years old. I am in a Sano-let. I am completely naked. My clothing is covered in feces. People keep knocking on the door, wondering when their turn to use the mobile receptacle will come. It is 1981. There are no cell phones. There is no Internet. Even H.A.M. radio technology sucks in this day and age. My parents, who frequently work late, have not arrived at the game. I am an island. My only company? A nearby island that looks exactly like me and revels in my embarrassment.

I did what I could to clean up. I wiped off my skin with toilet paper. I disposed of the fallen Speedo. My baseball socks, tight enough to receive the overflow from the Speedo were ruined. They were tossed as well.

My cleats were black. No problem. My socks were reasonable. My baseball pants, hit the hardest in the blast, were logically worse in the back than in the front. The legs were affected to the upper thigh.

My baseball jersey was flecked, but nothing that soaked through.

I dressed leaving my baseball shirt un-tucked. Luckily, one size was standard issue for the whole team. My shirt was ridiculously long for a 4'10" person. It could be stretched to mid thigh. Things were looking up. Not a disguise for the disaster that had just ensued but perhaps camouflage if I was lucky.

The question my brother asked me throughout my life was "Why didn't you just walk home?" The baseball field was located at the corner of Holly Street and Dry Creek Road. Our house was located off the corner of Holly Street and Crestline. Perhaps a 5-mile distance but a straight shot. And surely my parents, on the way to the game, would have picked me up and been humane to me. The real answer is that I never thought about going home. I only considered the tactics I would need for damage control to minimize my brother's inheritance of Juice from my misfortune.

And so, I went back to the dugout. I walked to the end of the bench, sat down, pulled the brim of my cap down low and said nothing. No one said a word. The game, an intense one run affair, was now in the third inning. Little League games last six innings. The game was half way over. Maybe, just maybe I could stick my head in the sand for three more innings.

It was then that my brother, my twin, my partner in soul ambled up and sat down right next to me. A future lawyer himself, he channeled Bobby Goren, Vincent D'Onofrio's character on the TV show Law and

Order: Criminal Intent. In fact, Goren could have learned a thing or two from Phil on matters regarding interrogation and psychological tactics.

Phil sat silently for about a minute, to settle in, let the tension build. Did he know what happened? Could he tell? Would he say anything?

"I saw you running before the first inning. Getting warmed up for the big game?" Phil eased in.

"I was just running," I mumbled

"That's good. That's good. We might need you. Division Championship. Big Game"

Like a cat toying with his prey he paused and sighed.

"What happened to your pants?" he said, barely containing a laugh. **Game on**. Phil knew what happened and he was going after the Juice, all of it. But he had to follow protocol. He had to be careful:

Twin law states the no Juice is earned from cruelty. That doesn't count. So Phil couldn't just blurt out "Ha Ha! Dave crapped in his pants!" It has to *happen* to your brother. He needed me to admit it and he needed someone else to notice.

"What happened to your pants, David?" he repeated.

"Leave me alone" I said

"I need to know what happened. What happened to your pants?" He said a bit more emphatically

Buckling under the pressure a bit I replied, "I fell in the mud"

Phil paused. *He had what he wanted.* A story he could disprove. A lie. And if I was lying, what was I hiding that was so much worse? He put his head in his hands and carefully considered how to handle it. How to gather the biggest Juice payload of his life.

"I can't figure it out." He whispered to himself, banging his palm against his forehead. "I just can't figure it out."

"What?" I asked

"It's 100 degrees in the shade. These fields are all dirt.

There's no grass. They don't water the dirt, David. So what I can't figure out is this: Where did you possibly find mud?" he spat, now not able to hold back laughter.

"I don't know" I said now unnerved.

"Where's the water, David? WHERE'S-THE-WA-TER?" he raised his eyebrows and annunciated slowly.

"Someone spilled their cooler" I said, clinging to my story.

Phil took a break. Maybe forty seconds. He mumbled to himself. "Someone spilled their cooler. You fell in the mud. That's too bad. That's bad luck."

Starting back in he hammered away, now with a sense of purpose. "You don't smell good, David. You don't smell good at all."

Phil finally got the help he was looking for when Brian Desmond, the only other kid paying attention asked

"Did you get sick and throw up?"

It took the lifeline and said. "Yeah. OK. I threw up."

Phil jumped in immediately. "So it wasn't mud. Why did you lie? Why didn't you just tell me? Why David? Why didn't you tell the truth?"

"I don't know", I said.

Phil kept the pressure on. He knew he was close but he wanted the right mental state before he went for a confession.

"Where are your baseball socks?"

"I didn't wear them today" I lied

"YES YOU DID, DAVID. YES . . . YOU . . . DID" he thundered.

"I saw you put them on. Where are your baseball socks?"

"I don't know. Leave me alone" I replied

"Did you throw them away" Phil said

"LEAVE ME ALONE!" I cried.

"I just want to know what happened" Phil retreated in a friendly tone.

Phil paused again. He was starting to draw attention and it was time for closing arguments. It was time to collect the Juice.

"People who throw up on themselves have stains down the front, on their shirt. Maybe the front of their pants" he posited.

"So?" Was the only thing I could think to say

"Soooooooooo . . . YOU have stains, horrible foul smelling stains, down the BACK of your pants and the BACK of your legs . . . . and your hat? How did you get it on your hat?"

A laugh from the peanut gallery signaled that my brother was gaining momentum. Endgame was near. Phil had the team's attention and was leading them down the primrose path. At some point, someone was going to accuse me of crapping my pants.

Manna rained from heaven as Brian Desmond said, "Did you throw up on the ground and fall in it?'

"I don't know" I said. Years of experience under the hot lights of Phil's interrogation had taught me never to admit to anything. Ever.

"You don't know?" said Phil incredulously. "You don't know?'

Phil knew that new line of reasoning was a blow to his argument. The psychological tactics would have to be escalated.

Lightly clapping his hands he laughed. At first lightly then hysterically. He could barely get the words out between fits of laughter.

"You don't know . . . . if it was mud or if you threw up . . . . or if you fell in it or where your baseball socks are or how in God's name you got stains ON YOUR HAT!!

HAHAHAHAHAHAHAHAHA!" he roared with laughter.

"WHAT DO YOU WANT FROM ME?" I yelled.

"I just want to know what happened," he said flippantly. "What happened, David?"

Phil waited for his accusation from the audience but none came.

Just then, out of the corner of my eye I saw salvation. My parents had arrived in their giant blue station wagon. Phil was out of time. In mere seconds my mother, the honorable Susan Nowick would be presiding over this investigation:

"Your honor, the witness is being badgered. I move that Phil's line of questioning be stricken from the record"

"Sustained!" She would bellow as the gavel came down. "One more word out of you Sir, and I'll hold you in contempt."

The jury would be hung.

I would become the O.J. Simpson of crapping in your pants. Guilty as sin, but I would never publicly admit to the crime.

NO JUICE FOR PHIL.

"If it doesn't fit you must acquit."

Then, the unthinkable happened. My Dad not my Mom approached the dugout. This couldn't be! He was a back of the bleachers type of parent. Hands off as far as sports went. He always waited until after the game to talk to us so we could concentrate. He waddled up and before even saying hello blurted past his moustache:

"What Happened? Did you shit your pants?"

The dugout erupted in laughter, coaches included. My Dad, a surgeon, direct in nature, could not understand what was so funny about his question.

Just like that, it was over. The Juice was in the bank. Phil had the look of someone who had just won the Powerball Lottery. So happy that it couldn't be real. For he had won the Lottery. The secret Lottery of twins.

I would never live the Astros incident down. Try as I might, I would never accumulate enough Juice to overcome that August day. Phil, as was his right, brought the incident to bear whenever he could. He spoke of it at prom. College friends reveled in telling me whenever the (Houston) Astros won. Family gatherings were Phil's favorite time to cast a sentimental reminder.

I asked my first wife to marry me on the eve of Thanksgiving at my parents' house. Immediately following, Phil insisted on a quick "secret meeting " with my new fiancé. The intimate and wonderful video from my second wedding ends unceremoniously with Phil yanking the cameraman aside and spitting out the tale. Phil paid for the video. Now I know why.

Yes, I believe my brother's only regret before his passing was that he would not be able to tell the Astros Incident to my 3 kids (Oz, ZaZa and Urijah) and share their laughter.

Why did it have to be that way? Why did I live and re-live this experience so many times?

Yehuda Berg (Co-Director of the Living Wisdom—Kabbalah Center) once said that, "Humiliation is very positive for the soul. Embarrassments, especially huge ones, therapeutically crush the ego." Everything you think you are, everything you think you have done diminishes. The BS is gone. There is nothing left but you. Then and only then can you see yourself as God sees you.

My brother loved seeing me as God sees me.

And he absolutely never got tired of it.

Namaste

STORY 4

WELCOME TO NEW MEXICO

If the person at the wheel refuses to ask for directions,
it is time for a new driver.
— *Jennifer Granholm*

I can generally tell the age of the high school wrestlers that I coach by their demeanors. If the wrestler is fourteen or fifteen years old, he acts a bit awkward, perhaps humbled by the leap from middle school to a larger pond. If the wrestler is eighteen years old, he displays an aura of relative calm (emphasis on relative); having scaled the Everest of adolescence, he is hopeful and a little bit daunted by the future as he glimpses adulthood. If the wrestler is between the ages of sixteen and seventeen, he is indestructible, and, above all, omnipotent. Absolute zero direction or advice from adults will penetrate his cerebral cortex for this two-year period; he already knows it all and will never die. No two individuals fit this mold more than the Nowick twins circa 1986. We had freshly minted driver's licenses and between us shared a souped-up vehicular absurdity known as the "Chin-Up Truck," a ridiculous homage to teenage excess and poor planning. Continuing on that theme, the Chin-Up Truck would also be our chariot in possibly the most ridiculous voyage of our wrestling careers: an unintentional trip to the great state of New Mexico.

The Chin-Up Truck started off as a solid, reliable Ford Bronco (preceding the OJ Simpson trial, this was still an acceptable means of transportation in America). It had been the family "snow" car for two years, and my father very generously offered to give the car to one twin and buy the other twin an equally priced used vehicle. So long as we maintained good grades, continued to stay out of trouble, and promised never to toilet paper Jodie Tucker's house again (a promise we could not possibly keep), our curfew would be extended to 10:30 p.m. and we would have unlimited driving privileges. In retrospect, what could this benign yet comically volatile man have been thinking?

My brother and I both had an idea of what mental processes were afoot in our father. Martin Nowick, MD, was and is to this day an unrestrained car buff. This quality resonated in my father, not out of greed or vanity, but out of historical context. My father is a chartered member of the "pull yourself up by the bootstraps" club. He was raised by his grandmother, a first generation Russian immigrant, after an incredibly messy divorce between his parents. Despite inheriting a squat, powerful, fighter's athleticism from his father (our Grandpa Sid), competing in sports was not an option for Martin. He worked no less than two after-school jobs at any one time, not for pocket cash, but to help keep a roof over his and his grandmother's heads. All of the popular kids at the fairly upscale Denver East High School had cool cars—T-Birds, Mustangs, Corvettes, all decked out and shiny—and it left an imprint on my dad. Thirty years later, having built a very successful medical practice with my mother, cars were an indulgence that Martin richly deserved.

As a result, like the sure-footed, amphibious birds in the movie *March of the Penguins*, my father would migrate to Murray Auto

Imports each year and trade his car in. Forget the fact that each of the cars probably had less than 10,000 miles on the odometer. My dad, armed with a full year of *Car and Driver* magazine under his belt, was primed to trade for a new vehicular soul mate with that new car smell and, more importantly, updated gadgetry. In preparation for sending the two of us to college (also an act of incredible generosity), my mother had banned my father from the car lot. His automotive heart was aching for novelty.

Sensing this opening, David and I hatched a scheme that was inspired by the single, resounding motivation of any sixteen or seventeen-year-old male: picking up hot chicks. It had been a long, dry romantic spell for the Nowick brethren. Despite achieving some real success for the Cherry Creek High School varsity wrestling team, we were commonly referred to as "those two wrestling dorks." Wrestling was not cool at Cherry Creek. Football was definitely cool. Donning androgynous dress and eyeliner (think Flock of Seagulls) was, for some reason, cool. White suits with pastel T-shirts (think *Miami Vice*) was absolutely, positively cool. But not wrestling. Wrestling was blue-collar, sweaty, and gross. Wrestling meant gaunt, sunken faces from weight-cutting, ringworm, and the smelliest, sweat-filled room (our wrestling room) in the universe.

Our wrestling dorkdom also did not mix well with several other sobering facts. We both stood about five feet tall. We both sported jailhouse crew cuts during wrestling season, administered by our athletic trainer, a hulking, codger of a man named Don Greibel (he had two crew cut hairstyling options in the Cherry Creek training room salon: "bald", or, as was our choice, "not bald"). Finally, as is the plight of all thirteen to fifteen-year-old boys, we had up to that point required the services of our mom to drive us everywhere. As a result, there existed all of the requisite formulae for a teenage dating black hole: not just the absence of hot chicks but what seemed like an irreversible negative void. The Chin-Up Truck, we hypothesized, would change everything.

It would provide us with the one solitary device that would enable us to create a wormhole in the hot chick space-time continuum: a killer car, one for the ages.

We thanked my dad profusely for the offer of two cars but served up a different plan. Could we perhaps share the Ford Bronco and invest the balance of whatever money he would have spent on another car in upgrades? Martin was intrigued; this was a wholly new vehicular experience that he had never contemplated. He had always bought new, everything factory-made. The Bronco could, in some ways, be his automotive opus, with his loyal sons at his side. Martin tried to feign indifference and told us he would think it over, but we knew we had him at "upgrades."

Why did the modified version of the Ford Bronco carry the moniker of the "Chin-Up Truck?" I'll get to that, but suffice it to say that the look that David and I were going for was vintage monster truck. We went through the list of renovations with my Dad: candy-apple red paint job, check; tastefully upgraded stereo, check; Yosemite Sam mud flaps— my dad though it a bit extravagant, but check. Two critical evolutionary items, in our view, were vetoed: the lift kit and the tires. All of the kids at Cherry Creek with similar jeeps or trucks had "jacked-up" their rides. This meant altering the suspension so the car sat much higher off the ground. Accordingly, much larger tires were required to offset this effect and for extreme off-road ventures on dry ground (in which we were not allowed to participate). Such alterations actually made the truck far less effective in snow and ice. The truck would be unusable in the winter, Dad said. What possible practical use would we have for a lift and giant tires? Like all sixteen-year-olds, we nodded our heads in agreement and immediately set about planning our insubordination.

The first trick was capital. How would we finance any additional upgrades that had to be paid for in cash? David and I had some allowance saved up, but using the skills of a future investment banker, I decided to tap into funds that were not technically mine but could be "invested" at my disposal and for my benefit. David and I would need to liquidate some bar bitzvah money— US Treasury bonds purchased by our maternal grandfather, which we damn well knew were meant for college. We would recoup our "investment" on the backside, at the resale of the truck in the future. Monetary intent of the family aside, I rightly pointed out to David that the bonds were indeed in our names and could be redeemed at any savings bank. Problem solved.

The second problem was trickier. How would we contract for the clandestine changes with our dad running the process? Using the skills of a future attorney, I decided to call the mechanic and string together a series of bald-faced lies. We had not mentioned a lift kit or giant tires because of budgetary constraints, I said on the phone to Don, of Don's Automotive in Littleton. We had agreed with our father that, if we paid for the new items separately and in cash, he would consent. Okay, Don said, how big a lift did we want? This is where our complete lack of automotive knowledge and common sense kicked in. Lifts and tires were measured in inches—24" this, 16" that, which all sounded so small. Feet or yards seemed like manlier units of measurement, but we could only choose from what was available, so we went with the biggest of both. "You sure," Don asked? Damn right we were sure. What did we look like, amateurs? He quoted us a price— quite economical compared to the total bond proceeds. We then inquired as to the largest size speakers we could buy with the remaining budget. He again blathered something in inches but emphasized that such speakers were "illegal in Littleton." We didn't live in Littleton, so no worries, we said.

Once we received the call from Don, we made certain to have a friend of ours drop us off to pick up the Bronco in our dad's absence. Since we only lifted the car a few inches, we reasoned that the changes would be subtle. Once our dad noticed, he would be slightly miffed at our mild rebellion, but he'd get over it. We approached Don's Automotive with the exuberance of, well, two kids about to get into their first car. Don spotted us, sauntered out to the parking lot, and shook his head. "We never done a lift that big; steering wheel has a little bit of play in it," he said. He hit the remote for the garage door, and in what seemed like movie-like slow motion, revealed an abomination.

The Bronco had morphed into something freakish; there was no other way to describe it. First, David and I had failed to do the requisite diligence on the meaning of the color "candy-apple red," which turned out to be a fantastic color for lip gloss, not so much for monster trucks. The truck's fuselage looked more appropriate for Charlie's Angels to pop out of for their latest mission, not for two supercool, stone-cold wrestlers to pick up hot chicks. The stereo, even at the lowest volume levels, was intolerable to the human eardrum. The speakers and equalizer consumed the *entire* back portion of the truck, leaving absolutely zero room for storage. The mutated bass— forgive my graphic description— literally made your rectum vibrate, not in a good way. Think about putting the sound system for your standard football stadium in the back of your car.

Most importantly, the lift was way, way too high. The truck towered comically like a steel praying mantis, which didn't bother either of us until we tried to get in. You have to understand that the Nowick family is essentially descended from a proud lineage of Hebrew hobbits. My mother stands 4'10" on a good day, my father a whopping 5'2". Our Grandpa Sid was the giant of the clan at 5'3", and his mother who emigrated from Russia was well below five feet. David and I were *seventeen years old* before we were taller than Willy the Whale, the menacing vertical gatekeeper for the roller coaster at Elitch Gardens Theme Park. I don't need to do the math for you. There was only one way for either of us to enter the truck without the assistance of an unbearably uncool stepladder. The driving twin was required to outstretch his Lilliputian arms to full length, grab onto the steering wheel, and hoist himself, utilizing upper body strength, into the driver's seat. He would then need to migrate to the passenger side of the vehicle and give his brother a boost from above. Hence the name, the "Chin-Up Truck."

Driving the car was also a challenging (and dangerous) enterprise. As Don had mentioned, the steering wheel had a "little bit of play" in it. This euphemistically meant the steering mechanism could be twisted an entire quarter turn, left or right, and the car would not veer a single inch. It was like playing some sort of broken arcade game on live roads. After getting the initial hang of it, we thanked Don for his hard work and drove home, somewhat fearful of our dad's reaction.

Furious does not begin to describe Martin's condition upon first glimpsing the truck. He was, quite literally, hopping mad. I've briefly mentioned the magnanimous qualities of my father: generosity, a tireless work ethic (he literally worked twenty-four hours a day as an OBGYN physician), an innate affability, the desire to provide his children with anything and everything he never had, etc. But my father also had, at the right moments in time, a mercurial streak that resembled Homer Simpson's comically explosive temperament— my lord, was it funny, and scary. Martin started out by dashing a full lap around the Chin-Up Truck and shouting out his own home-brewed list of obscenities that all began with the prefix "rat" (rat-f'ing, rat-shit, or combos like rat-f'ing-bastard, to name a few). Upon completion of this semicircle of rage, he immediately removed his belt and began swinging the buckle above his head like a ninja. Martin had long since given up corporal punishment as we grew older, primarily because our full-grown, thick skulls began to hurt his surgeon's hands. Nevertheless, this desecration of the Ford Bronco called for a revival of police brutality. David and I cleared out like scared antelope, Martin playing the role of the belt-wielding cheetah. The two of us caught a couple of stray whacks from the belt as we zigged and zagged around our cul-de-sac, and my mom intervened as growing numbers of neighbors gathered to watch this calamity unfold. Weeks passed, and my father could not bear to speak to either of us. Although creating an initial buzz at school, the Chin-Up Truck failed to produce even a single glance from a hot chick, and eventually the height differential between twins and truck began to draw comparisons to clowns jumping out of the stilted car at Barnum & Bailey Circus. We had now graduated from "those two wrestling dorks" to "those two wrestling dorks with that weird truck."

In absence of any foreseeable glasnost on the family front, we looked forward to the spring wrestling season as a diversion. I was fresh off my first trip to the state finals (I lost a heartbreaker in overtime) and felt sure that I was now destined for NCAA and Olympic greatness. We huddled with our high school coach, Steve Foster, to map out logistically which tournaments he believed we should attend between the months of March and July. David and I had progressed to the point where several national-level tournaments in Las Vegas, Nebraska, Iowa, etc., were now competitive options for the two of us. As Coach Foster reviewed the schedule, he looked us in the eyes, paused, and uttered one simple phrase: "If you boys really want to find out how good you are, go down to Rocky Ford."

We knew exactly what he meant. Rocky Ford is a small community in rural southeastern Colorado (population in 1986 was around 2,500) known for two things: they are the self-proclaimed "Sweet Melon Capitol of the World" owing to the town's lifeblood and agricultural prize, melons, and, at the time, Rocky Ford boasted the finest wrestling team in Colorado. Rocky Ford had won an endless string of state titles in the Colorado 3A division— for smaller schools. (Such classifications, based on school size, mean far less in competitive balance for wrestling than they do in other sports. That is one of my favorite aspects of the sport; wrestling is often a shining source of pride for small towns, and they frequently end up beating the tar out of their big city counterparts. The sport requires far less logistics, equipment, and investment than, say, football. All you need is a pair of shoes, a decent-size wrestling mat, three to four solid workout partners, a good coach, and you will go far). Rocky Ford was coached by the legendary but somewhat free-spirited Charlie White. As an embodiment of their coach, the Fighting Meloneers' (yes that was their team's nickname) wrestling style encouraged risk:

high amplitude throws (some of their wrestlers made the US World Team in Greco-Roman), spectacular circus moves, and breathtaking rolls. Indeed, Charlie White and his Meloneers had created not just a successful wrestling program, but a cult legend in Colorado sports.

Because of their remote location, the wrestlers from Rocky Ford rarely faced off against the urban powerhouses to the north. They would simply swoop into the Denver Auditorium Arena once a year and take the place by storm, and poof, outside of residents in the extreme south of the state of Colorado, you never saw them again until the next year. For this reason, the tiny town of Rocky Ford held an annual tournament in the spring that, to this day, is incredibly well-attended. The saying was that "Rocky Ford doesn't come to you. You go to Rocky Ford." That is exactly what Coach Foster was driving at. Rocky Ford had a string of three phenomenal lightweights, all around the same size. Each had won a state championship at 98, 105 and 112 pounds, respectively, but according to our Coach (he had called Charlie White to confirm), all three would be competing at 114.5 pounds (my weight), the Olympic classification of fifty-two kilograms. Coach Foster was a master motivator by nature and drew on every source of inspiration possible: negative reinforcement, positive reinforcement, fear, humor, inspirational quotes, Knute Rockne like prematch pep talks, silence— you name it. He knew how to dial into each kid individually and drag the best out of him, even if his best came out kicking and screaming. Without a note of criticism, his straightforward comment was a naked challenge to the two of us. Were we as good as we thought? Did we deserve all the attention we received from local sports reporters? (The "identical twin" angle story never wore off. Two local-interest news articles and one TV spot about us as sheer novelty had already been produced). If so, prove it. Coach Foster did not need to say a word more; we were already mentally packing up for Rocky Ford.

On a Friday, sometime mid-April, we prepared for our voyage, and each of us had a few pounds to sweat off. We ate sparingly that day, and after school, concocted the brilliant idea of converting our downstairs bathroom into a steam spa. For two hours, the shower poured at full-blast hot. We both donned rubber suits that gave us the appearance of spacemen. We had a nice little routine going. One twin would stand and execute jumping jacks on the bathroom floor while the other sat on the toilet and rocked back and forth like a Hasidic Rabbi deep in prayer. All the while we were sweating profusely. At approximately four p.m., the weight-cutting was done, and the downstairs was a dripping, sweaty, mildew-ravaged disaster. We looked around at the damage. Too late now— we needed to get on the road and it was a long drive (weigh-ins ended at 11:00 p.m.). We would face the consequences on Sunday when we returned, and who knew, it was just water. Maybe it would dry.

We fired up the truck, our gear piled in on top of the speakers, and headed off. We made it about halfway down the street when Martin exploded out of the front door in his bathrobe, fresh off his own after-work hot shower. It was a cold April afternoon— the last grips of the Rocky Mountains winter— and I swear that I saw steam emanating off Martin's bald pate. We had a choice: stop the car and face the consequences for destroying our bathroom or step on the gas and never look back. We chose that latter, but my father did not give up easily. His bedroom slippers slapping against the pavement, Martin gave chase at sprinter's speed for at least a full block. Here was the absolute travesty to this already repugnant display of behavior on our part: our dad had not, in fact, discovered the bathroom debacle (he later freaked out completely). As an olive branch to resolve the whole truck situation, Martin had stopped by AAA and bought a special roadmap that gave specific directions to Rocky Ford, a map we would later sorely need. He was running after us with all his might, dressed like a Roman emperor in terrycloth, to make sure his sons got to their destination safely and on time. As he finally exhausted his run and saw our truck disappear on the horizon, the map remained tucked in his robe pocket. Lord, forgive us; I cringe to this day.

We hit US Interstate 25, Colorado's state-long north/south thoroughfare, with a vengeance. Genesis's *ABACAB* played in the deafening back speakers—it was our first big road trip, our first time away from home with no supervision, our first time (of many to come) getting horribly lost. We didn't know it at the time (because our mother drove us everywhere in all instances prior), but sense of direction is not a Nowick strong suit. To this day, both David and I can manage, somehow, to lose our way with modern gear such as GPS, Google maps, etc., even if we have been to our destination before. In 1986, no such technology existed, just the plain old roadmap. This simple tool, for some inexplicable reason in our sixteen-year-old heads, was a useless annoyance. We had been to Rocky Ford before when we were thirteen for an age group nationals training camp. Forget the fact that we slept the entire way as our mom chauffeured us to our destination; we knew, without having to look at any stupid map, that Rocky Ford was very far south, just a mile or two off I-25 South. If we drove far enough south on I-25, signs would eventually point the way. Not so much …

The correct way to reach Rocky Ford from Denver has a very simple added step, a step that any moron with an IQ above fifty could ascertain from looking at a roadmap or simply stopping and asking for directions, but not us. Yes, you drive a good distance south on I-25 to Pueblo, but then you hit a dead left on US 50 for fifty-three miles, and it takes you straight to your destination.

As we reached Colorado Springs, we switched the music from Genesis to Prince— *Purple Rain*. As if some curse from the angered wrestling gods kicked in, the album's title song conjured buckets of freezing sleet from the heavens. Visibility was less than zero and we started to learn that the suspension lift on the truck and gorilla tires indeed did make the car worthless in bad weather. Twice on standard highway turns we could feel the tires slip, which to any driver but a sixteen-year-old boy would dictate reducing speed. We did not. We may have been beginner drivers, but we weren't sissies for Pete's sake.

I began to lose my nerve when we hit Pueblo. Countless semitrucks zoomed by and shook the Chin-Up Truck off course. The frozen rain and hail only worsened as we progressed. I first jokingly, and then very seriously, suggested to David that we bag the whole road trip and hit Hy's Burger Stand in Pueblo. David, being just slightly more morally grounded and responsible than I, refused, and the disagreement turned into a full-fledged argument. "We are almost there," he said. "It isn't far past Pueblo. Just pipe down." I relented, and we drove on— and on, and on, and on. Two hours passed as we continued to careen down I-25. The rain clouds persisted in menacing us every step of the way. It was near impossible to see the names on the road signs as we sped by. A vicious debate broke out. "We passed it. Turn around." "No we didn't. We are not stopping; we are almost there." The amusing part of the quarrel was that David and I, like two jousting British barristers playing both sides of the coin for sport, would alternate views. First he would insist that we turn around. "No way," I would reply. "Okay, I'm sure we passed it," I would bemoan a few minutes later. "We've come too far; we can't turn back," he would retort. Not once did a slightly altered view enter the argument, that of simply stopping and asking for directions. Finally, a road sign that we could see clearly emerged. The sign bore a message with a large yellow flag/red symbol in the middle. David, focusing on the road, whined, "What did that sign say?" I didn't reply at first. Instead, I let out a primordial scream at the top of my lungs. "The sign said 'Welcome to New Mexico,' you SOB!"

This is the power of adolescent obstinacy. My brother and I, both future Stanford grads, had somehow managed not only to arrive at the wrong destination but also to drive to the wrong *state*— and the idiocy continued. My brother leapt from the car into the driving rain and started shrieking like a banshee in frustration; I followed suit. As we wailed to the heavens, I stomped toward my brother and snatched the keys from his hands. "You drove us to the wrong state, you moron," I said, and an impromptu wrestling match ensued. My brother shot a single-leg takedown and drove me into the mud on the shoulder of the road. I countered quickly with a rolling reversal maneuver and gained the advantage, but David was a step ahead of me. He leapt to his feet, turned, spun, and delivered a brilliant five-point headlock that created an audible mud splash on impact. I was momentarily stunned (and impressed), and I lay still in the muck, covered head to toe in sludge like an aborigine in parachute pants. The fight was over— David had wrested the keys from me. I had lost this round, but I would find a way to win the war when we returned to the red-matted wrestling room at Cherry Creek. I would invent an entirely new array of cheap shots and sucker punches for my twin. I heard the Chin-Up Truck start and began to waddle back in defeat. And then, he drove away. My brother, with whom I shared a womb and 99 percent of my DNA, with whom I had spent every day of my life, with whom I had fought side by side on the playgrounds of Greenwood Elementary School, abandoned me like roadkill on the New Mexico state line.

Stunned, I again channeled the skills of a future attorney; I plotted my next steps and David's personal and criminal demise. First, I needed to hitchhike to Pueblo and clear my head at Hy's Burger Stand. I would order the quadruple (Hy's was the only burger joint in Colorado to offer an actual quadruple burger on the menu); I deserved it. Second, I would notify the authorities that I had been recklessly abandoned in a pouring rainstorm by my brother. That had to be a major crime of some sort. From the payphone at Hy's I would immediately alert the authorities—first the local police and then the FBI. The very fact the he deposited me across the state line made it a federal case; I knew that much. I would then call and notify my parents that David was (a) the sole culprit of the bathroom disaster and (b) a fugitive from justice. I would strongly urge my parents to cooperate with the authorities in order to ensure David would come to no harm during his apprehension. At his trial, I would act as a rare mix of star witness for the prosecution and, at sentencing, character witness for the defense. I had just seen Scan

Penn's *Bad Boys*, which graphically depicted life in a juvenile detention center, so although making damn sure my brother would not roam the streets anytime soon, abandoning people at random in that preposterous truck, I would plead for leniency. I was a big enough man to help with his rehabilitation in the minimum security halfway house and would visit often, bringing newspaper clippings of my wrestling exploits and perhaps even some of Coach Foster's motivational quotes and speeches for him to read in his vast spare time. He would never wrestle again, of course, but he would recover someday and become a better man for the experience. I would even allow him to sit in my corner at the 1992 Olympics; that would help heal his pain.

I woke up from my delusions of grandeur to find the Chin-Up Truck idling behind me on the road's shoulder—my brother at the helm, his face also streaked with mud. In the very first mature decision of his life (it would be years before I experienced the same), he had driven down the highway to a filling station, refueled the truck, purchased a road map, and asked for directions. Several backroad options existed that might have been a quicker fix to get to Rocky Ford, but we opted for the much safer bet. Reverse course and head north on I-25 to Pueblo and hit a hard right on US 50 to Rocky Ford.

We arrived in Rocky Ford just before the closing of weigh-ins. The remaining officials at the high school ogled us with a mix of fear and curiosity as we removed our mud-sodden clothes. Long story, we said. As we exited the building, we were famished and weary. We began canvassing Rocky Ford's limited streetscape looking for someplace, anyplace, to eat. The rain had relented, and it seemed as if the wrestling Gods had made their point. Better times lay ahead, until …

A police cruiser that looked like a leftover prop from *Mayberry R.F.D.* flashed its single light. My brother and I both lay our heads on the dash in utter defeat. The smalltown cop sauntered toward us at a sober pace. In retrospect, I can imagine his motivations. Two kids, roaming around town at eleven forty-five at night in some sort of modified red tractor, Denver plates—we'll see about this. My brother rolled down the window, and the middle-aged man could not hide his shock at our mud-caked faces. He jettisoned the standard "License and registration, please" for "What in the hell is wrong with you boys?" My brother began a long diatribe about our perilous journey, a speech that warranted zero sympathy until he dropped the magic phrase: " … and we are wrestlers in town for the tournament." Bingo. The officer's face immediately lit up. "Aw, you boys are wrestlers. Why didn't you say so!" he cried. He had been a champion himself back in the day and had wrestled on Charlie White's first state championship team. We asked him if any dining establishments remained open, and we received a police escort to Rocky Ford's only late-night diner. (To this day, I continue to be amazed at the kinship our sport offers—bottle it and mix it in the water supply, and we might save the world). The officer shook our hands as if we shared a secret bond—which we did—and offered a word of parting advice. "You boys should clean up," he said. We planned to.

We entered the Rocky Ford gym the next morning ready for battle and immediately checked the brackets. My bracket read like a *Who's Who* of high school lightweight wrestling. Apparently I was not alone in my desire to test my skills against the Rocky Ford trio. Two additional state champions from Colorado, as well as top-ranked wrestlers from New Mexico and Kansas, had made the pilgrimage. I slugged out three wins in the morning before getting my chance at the first, and lightest, of the Meloneer gladiators. I was warming up for the match, a bit hesitant. This was one of the unmistakable moments unique to wrestling or boxing or other combative sports; I was about to find the truth. *How good was I?* In other sports, one might point to the weather, teammates, coach's game plan, etc., as possible havens for excuse. No such luxury in wrestling.

At that moment, the most amazing thing happened. The beautiful Angela appeared matside and spoke to me like, well, an Angel. "Is that your truck outside?" she asked. "Yes, well … (I was about to explain that I shared it with my brother but chose to omit that fact) yes," I stuttered. "You're good. I saw you downstate (the high school state tournament)," she said in a slight, charming Latina accent (pronounced with a slight intonation at the end). Having developed zero dating skills at that point, I openly gawked. Angela's young build, a seventeen-year-old mix of Italian and Spanish, could most accurately be described as explosive. "Th-Thanks," I said, and a revelation hit me in the head like a ton of bricks. Like Einstein with his theory of general relativity, I had broken the code in the hot chick universe—the answer was small towns. Wrestling was cool in small towns; weird cars and, preferably, trucks were cool in small towns. In fact, I had heard of a practice called "cruising," in which the smalltown locals traversed on a nightly basis up and down Main Street to the only stoplight, turned around at the Dairy Queen, and repeated the process again and again. I just had not yet drawn the connection. From that point on, my brother and I traveled to as many small town wrestling tournaments as possible, like a wrestling traveling road show. We would shed our personas as *über*geeks in Cherry Creek and leap into an alternative reality, conversing with as many smalltown girls (who were infinitely more grounded and nicer) as we were able.

Back to Angela. As she had a brother competing at the tournament, she was quite knowledgeable. "This guy's good; he's a state champ (said as one word, with emphasis at the end—"stet*champ*"), she said about my next opponent. "Tell you what, if you win, I'll give you my phone number." Poor guy, he never had a chance …

Long story short, neither David nor I emerged as the champion of the tournament that day, but we both came home with medals. More importantly, we got our licks in against the best of the best. I did indeed receive Angela's phone number, and we dated long-distance, Pueblo to Denver, for a brief period. My brother and I essentially split the state into two with regard to hot chicks and small towns. David began dating a girl (with whom he made acquaintance at a wrestling tournament) from

Broomfield, in the north, and I continued to mine the south—Douglas County and below. We returned home from Rocky Ford to a fuming mother and father, but as they say, the journey made it all worth the while.

Several morals to this story exist. If you have one or more sons, please try diligently to forget every single thing they say or do between the ages of sixteen and seventeen. They are guilty by reason of hormonal insanity. It eventually wears off. Second, no matter your age, a little direction from your mentors or elders never hurt anyone. Taking some extra time to plot your course before leaping is actually a good thing. Finally, never paint anything, I mean anything, candy-apple red.

Namaste.

STORY 5

THE GREATEST STATE TOURNAMENT EVER

Excellence is an art won by training and habituation.
We do not act rightly because we have virtue or excellence,
but we rather have those because we have acted rightly.
We are what we repeatedly do. Excellence, then, is not an act
but a habit. — **Aristotle**

No single quote rings truer in relation to the positive results that I have encountered in my life than Aristotle's sage advice listed above. I first read the above quote in a college philosophy class, but I really didn't understand its wisdom until I heard the same message repeated in a more modern vernacular. Author Dan Coyle, in his book *The Talent Code*, says it this way: "Genius: it's not who you are but *what you do*." He proposes that Mozart, Einstein, and Tiger Woods garner their achievements not from a degree of divine talents, but from the ability to focus for long periods of time, the presence of one or more exacting mentors, and some type of personal experience that hit home at an early age to spark a drive bordering on obsession.

I use the words "positive results" above, because, in my opinion, we can distinguish such achievements from what I would view as true success. Thus, while I agree that achieving excellence and genius is primarily based on our repetitive actions, I also believe that attaining true joy, true triumph, and true success arises more from *how* such positive results are achieved. Famed Yogi Bryan Kest probably expressed it best when he said, "It's not what you do in [my yoga classes], but *how* you do what you do." I feel certain that all of the aforementioned virtuosos embodied this quality as well. But in my experience and, I'm sure, yours, we have all encountered somewhat soulless, unhappy, or lost individuals who have achieved many positive results and ruined their lives in the process. To me, the measuring stick in this regard is not the actual result of our aspirations, but whether we enjoyed the journey.

On that note, I want to tell you about the greatest state high school wrestling tournament I ever saw any competitor experience. The wrestler was my twin brother, David—he placed sixth in the 112-pound weight division in 1987. "Sixth place?" you ask. What could possibly be so notable about finishing behind five other guys that would warrant such acclamation? "Possibly nepotism or family bias on my part," you say. But the remarkable element of his performance is this fact: he did it less than fourteen weeks after shattering—not breaking, *shattering*—his left fibula. Aside from my brother (armed with fanatical perseverance), four exceptional people really made it happen: a brilliant surgeon, our high school coach, his son, and a fast-talking Iowa Hawkeye legend.

Before delving into the experience, let me rewind to one year prior where the table was set. As a high school sophomore, David was steamrolling his way to his first state medal in the quarterfinals of the 1986 state tournament. (David had made a tremendous physical sacrifice in order to lose enough bodyweight to wrestle in the 105-pound division. He began the season wrestling at 112 pounds and had the look of an Olympic athlete. As was common practice at the time, he made the "Christmas Drop" in weight division to 105 pounds, transforming his look to that of a starving refugee). He carried a six-point lead in this crucial match with less than thirty seconds left on the clock. Minutes before, I had easily won my own quarterfinal match in the weight division below, securing my second state medal in as many years of competition. But I was even more thrilled for my brother, who had worked so hard. Standing matside, I beamed with pride and shared a few premature backslaps with our high school coach, Steve Foster.

The ensuing thirty seconds—the duration of the match—was a mix of horror and surrealism. It began with a ghastly error in strategy on my brother's part. David began on top (or riding) position, and his opponent had briefly flashed a desperation reversal maneuver designed to roll my brother to his back and achieve a pin—the only plausible victory scenario achievable in thirty seconds (or so we thought). In order to avoid such a disaster, my brother decided to concede an easy two-point reversal, leaving his opponent on top. His rationale was that, with a four-point lead and twenty-five seconds left, he could "table out" and avoid being pinned quite easily, making such a tactic the safest bet. In an act of pure capitulation, he lowered himself to his stomach, buried his head in the mat, and spread his arms wide like a crocodile sunning himself on the Louisiana bayou. His thought process was faulty for two reasons: he forgot a) where he was (at the state tournament, where the excitement of the crowd often tempts referees to insert themselves as an active part of the show instead of leaving it to the wrestlers) and b) where he came from (we hailed from the lily-white, suburban, athletic powerhouse, Cherry Creek High School—the school everyone, most notably the predominantly blue-collar crowd, loved to hate). David received an exuberant warning for "stalling" (a penalty for passivity) from the referee within five seconds. Because of his prone position and the crowd's noise, David could not hear or see the referee, and he gave the appearance that he was openly ignoring the man. Five seconds later, David was dinged with his first one-point penalty for the same foul. He remained stone-like in his reptilian defense strategy. Five seconds later, the visibly angered referee added another one-point stalling penalty. Ten seconds remained in the match. Coach Foster shouted at the top of his lungs to David that he was being penalized at a rapid-fire rate. At this point, my brother lifted his head from the mat in a slight state of confusion, but he didn't seem worried. Time expired, and my brother regained his feet in jubilance, his arms triumphantly raised in the air. The referee had made his point, it seemed, but it appeared as if David had escaped the match with a two-point victory and his first state medal. Not so fast.

I will never forget the moment that followed for as long as I live; David and I each still have nightmares reenacting some version of the act. With David's back turned to the referee as he headed toward our corner for a victory embrace, the referee paused, assumed a contemplative look, and raised two fingers in the air in defiance. I didn't understand what the hand signal meant, but Coach Foster, a veteran of over thirty years of wresting, knew all too well. In wrestling, your third caution for stalling is worth two points. The referee had decided to alter the actual match after its conclusion. He retroactively awarded David's opponent his *fourth* penalty point within a span of twenty-five seconds. Because my brother was not facing the referee and did not see this travesty, Coach Foster was forced to break (or more accurately, physically shake) the news to David that the match was not over. The score was now tied and the match would proceed to overtime. My brother began vehemently arguing with both of us. What were we talking about? The match was over, he had won. We were literally forced to push him to the middle of the mat to continue. He was stunned to the point of paralysis and crumbled in front of us. He was beaten handily in this synthetic overtime by his newly fired-up opponent (giddy at his second chance at life in the state tournament) and subsequently made a quick exit in the consolation rounds. We were all sick. David would have to wait and work for another entire year for a medal. Any athlete that has completed the requisite training in the span of a wrestling season knows this is a painful eternity. David was forced to sit—stunned and broken—in the stands and watch his twin brother (me) move on to the state finals, an accomplishment on my part that added—in a perverse, sibling-comparison way—to his pain.

Upon exiting from the 1986 state tournament, David immediately began his offseason program by plunging into an Al Gore-like, depression-induced eating binge and embracing a change in appearance/wardrobe. In the month following the tournament, David proceeded to balloon from 105 to the neighborhood of 135 pounds—hardly flattering on his five-foot frame. Impossible, you say? One only need to watch Morgan Spurlock's shocking documentary *Super Size Me*, in which the filmmaker ate McDonald's cuisine for breakfast, lunch and dinner for one solid month, ordering the largest portions possible, and basically ruined his health. David's regimen was not too dissimilar. McDonald's for breakfast, Burger King for lunch, Dairy Queen as an after-school snack, and birthday cake for dinner. (Our relatives, at the behest of our mother, collectively sent us eleven—yes, eleven—birthday cakes since we were unable to eat a crumb of food at our own family birthday party on February 5). He also decided to change his look. This was 1986 and the "mullet" (short and spiked hair on top, long in back, down to the shoulders—think Canadian hockey player) reigned supreme as the teenage hairstyle of the times. My brother and I both pined for a mullet, but because we both had short, somewhat wavy hair, the hairstyle was a natural impossibility. So my brother decided for the next best thing: a perm—a perm gone horribly wrong. Why he decided on this hairstyle, I will never know, but he showed up at our home one day looking like a bloated George Washington (sans the white baby powder). I laughed uncontrollably. I couldn't help it. He was so mortified that he took to wearing a French beret everywhere to cover this abomination. Why a French beret? Your guess is as good as mine—it was the 80's. Additionally, my brother had outgrown (horizontally) all of his school clothes, and my parents were not about to pacify him by getting him a newer, fatter wardrobe. Instead, everywhere he now went, my brother sported one of two stretchable, velour FILA sweat suits that our Grandpa Sid had purchased for us in Israel. Thus, David walked the halls of the ultra-trendy Cherry Creek High School looking like a portly Armenian gangster for the duration of the 1986 school year.

Despite his newly challenged build, the spring and summer wrestling season (the offseason period in which American wrestlers compete individually in freestyle and Greco-Roman) showed some odd promise for David. He was forced to compete at weight classes one or two divisions above his usual competitve weight (123- to 130-pound) yet, surprisingly, held his own against much larger and stronger wrestlers who were highly ranked. He still looked comically dumpy in his singlet and was forced to shed the French beret for competition. For the first time in my life, people, instead of chronically confusing our identities, started asking if we were related.

Then came summer wrestling camp at the University of Iowa. In case you are wondering, the heroic portion of the story begins now. David's shape had gradually improved and his hair relaxed a bit. The velour sweat suits, now threadbare from overuse, had been jettisoned. The camp was a two-week "intensive" training experience at the University of Iowa, headed by wrestling legend Dan Gable. The Iowa Hawkeye program was fresh off another NCAA title, and to this day, it carries a reputation similar to that of Alabama in football—diehard and storied. The gold standard wrestler of the eighties for the Hawkeyes was a dynamic 126-pounder named Barry Davis. He exuded an intensity and energy that would come to define modern Iowa wrestling, and he used this attribute to win several NCAA championships, world medals, and a spot on the 1988 Olympic team. The two of us idolized Barry Davis, and we were thrilled to attend one of his technique sessions at the camp. At the conclusion of Davis's instruction, my brother approached him and asked for an autograph (not a common request for amateur wrestlers). Davis laughed jovially, embraced my brother in a jubilant bear hug, and made an incredibly gracious offer. "I can do better than that, buddy. I'll be training at 7:00 a.m. tomorrow. Why don't you two drop by, and I'll help you however I can." What a *mensch*. We did as instructed, showing up at Carver-Hawkeye Arena at six the next morning, just to be sure. That morning is easily one of my favorite adolescent memories. We spent an hour with Barry, and he simply asked us to wrestle and drill for five minutes so he could observe. To this day, I have never met another competitor or coach better at immediately diagnosing a wrestler's style, strengths, and weaknesses. (Barry is currently the head coach of the University of Wisconsin and continues to work his magic). Barry Davis is a type of wrestling savant, and like many men with a touch of genius, Barry expressed ideas for the next fifty-five minutes in rapid succession, most often in fragments. Advice poured out of his consciousness with such speed and efficiency that punctuation or pauses would only have suppressed such brilliance. He ended the session by giving us both his address and phone number and told us, "If you ever need my help, just call or write." What a guy—an Olympian offering two random high school kids from Colorado such generosity. True story. We walked out of the brief meeting sky-high, and my brother subconsciously made a seminal decision. He decided to make the transition from awkward kid to admirable young man.

I would not reach such a point of maturity, unfortunately, until several years later, and I proceeded to prove it as we returned from Iowa camp in late July. Thoroughly exhausted from a solid year of wrestling (and chronically losing weight), I decided to be a normal kid for a couple of months—live the good life of a teenager. I relaxed my diet, hung out with my doe-eyed high school sweetheart, and did not lace up my wrestling shoes until October. Conversely, my brother packed up and spent the next two months at the University of Southern Colorado, working out with their college wrestling team. He crashed on various college wrestlers' couches like some sort of grappling hobo. He trained twice a day with everybody and anybody that was willing. I didn't see him for the duration of the summer, and unbelievable rumors were soon floating back to Denver that some high school kid was the best lightweight on their team. David returned for the school year with a chiseled physique, beaming with confidence.

Entering the 1986-87 high school season, the Cherry Creek lineup at the lower weights was devastating. I was ranked number one at 105 pounds. My brother was number one at 112. Above us, at 119 pounds and also ranked number one, was a young man named Scott Gates, possibly the most spectacular high school wrestler I have ever seen in Colorado (I've been wrestling and coaching in the state for twenty years). He had won state titles both his freshman and sophomore years, capitalizing on years of wrestling experience and freakish athletic gifts. Our high school was a suburban football factory and boasted several 200–pound-plus players that would soon play Division I football. Scott, walking around at 125–130 pounds, routinely embarrassed even the strongest football players in the weight room, and he held the overall bench press and squat records for our school by a long shot. For fun, he decided to join the players in their end-of-summer athletic testing and also proved to be the fastest athlete in the school. As somewhat of an afterthought, Coach Foster's son, Jason, would also matriculate to our program as a freshman that year. Jason had attended a private Catholic academy for grade school and middle school and was painfully shy and incredibly polite. Being a coach's son, he had been wrestling from a very young age and could hold his own with anybody, but he would have trouble cracking our lineup at the lightweights. Word was that, despite Jason's having the ability to start for any other high school team, Coach Foster would place his son at his natural weight, 119 pounds, on the junior varsity, under the great Scott Gates. The plan was that Jason was to gain seasoning for the year by wrestling his older, more accomplished teammates and then go on to a stellar career (which he did).

My brother's progression did not hit home for me until late October, 1986, on our first day of wresting practice for the new high school season. Once our drills and calisthenics had ended, it was time for "live" practice wrestling. Like an old-western desperado, David walked straight up to Scott Gates, shook hands, and scored two takedowns in rapid succession. Up to that point, I can't remember either of us scoring a single point on Gates in the five years prior. My brother then turned his attention to Jason and began racking up points with an array of moves I had never seen. A disturbing thought entered my head: my twin brother, to whom I had always been compared so closely, was now a better wrestler than I—much better. My brother's reign of terror continued for two more days in the Cherry Creek wrestling room. His technique and tempo were electric. I have no doubt in my mind that David— the wrestler that he was at that specific moment in time— would have powered his way to a state title that year and possibly gone on to another. Neither of us would wrestle better, ever, than my brother did for that brief period of time (we continued in the sport for the better part of ten years). Then it all changed. Just like that, it all changed ...

On the fourth day of practice, David, having trouble garnering a fair match with the lightweights, paired up with a brutish 145-pounder, Jim Wonhoff, and proceeded to handle our larger teammate with perfect technique and stunning speed. In a moment of frustration and slight embarrassment, Jim (who would fittingly become a world-class jujitsu black belt) hit an unorthodox move with all of his sizeable strength and pulled my brother down from behind. The crack was audible from ten feet away.

An ever so brief moment of silence ensued, and then my brother let out a bloodcurdling scream. His left ankle elevated in the air and grossly contorted, my brother cried like a scared infant for what seemed like forever. Everybody in the room froze, and it was the only time I can remember Coach Foster ending practice prematurely. He wanted everybody out of the room as quickly as possible. The next few hours were blurry. There was an ambulance ride, X-rays confirming that my brother's fibula had splintered into many pieces, the inevitable announcement from the junior resident doctor that his wrestling season (and possibly career) was over, and … crying. Lots of soul-crushing, agonizing, embittered crying. Wrestling was everything to David, and according to the initial diagnosis, he would have to endure yet another year of pain to gain redemption, best case scenario. A five-hour surgery followed, performed by a prestigious doctor who worked on the Denver Broncos' football players for all matters orthopedic. My father, a tenured physician at the hospital, pulled those strings.

The following morning, the surgeon had more encouraging news and assuaged my brother's fears. David's wrestling career was, indeed, not over. The doctor confidently proclaimed that David would be able to make a full recovery by the following season. My brother was devastated. The next day he was discharged to go home, and the phone rang as he walked through the door. It was his own physician who had seen him immediately after the accident. "How are you?" he inquired. When David told him that wrestling would not be possible for another year, Dr. Tschetter said, "I want you to see a special sports doctor to consult about your rehabilitation." The next week David visited Dr. Mack. After reviewing the medical records and taking more extensive X-Rays, the doctor told David that he would heal like new. He then mentioned offhand, "Heck, we've even had some of the Broncos come back the same season with an Aircast." David's ears perked up. Was it feasible to come back this season? he asked. "For wrestling," replied the doctor, "I'm not sure how good your performance would be." Undaunted, David restated the question more specifically: performance issues aside, was it *possible* to resume wrestling in the ensuing months and not reinjure the ankle? "I guess, if you put it that way, the answer is yes," the doctor said. That was all David needed to hear. He marked January 15, one month before the 1987 state tournament— ten weeks from then—as his target return date. He was instructed to use crutches everywhere; no weight was to be put on the ankle until February, save his hypothetical return to the wrestling mat.

My brother began his rehabilitation immediately, the second he returned home from the doctor's office. The doctor prescribed fifty leg lifts per day with a device made from surgical tubing. David did 200 per day. David asked the high school trainer what form of exercise would most closely match the cardiovascular requirements of wrestling. "Swiming, most likely," the trainer replied. My brother swam like a fish, one hundred laps per day. Dr. Mack mentioned that studies had shown evidence that increased muscle mass and strength in the *other* leg had some sort of transference effect that promoted healing, so David got up at 6:00 a.m. to train with a local bodybuilder and did one-legged lifts, as well as a rigorous upper body routine. In addition to using crutches everywhere, he was supposed to elevate his leg at all times, and much to the chagrin of teachers and our parents, his leg never left a table or desk while he was resting. As January 15 drew closer, we began to believe (somewhat unrealistically) that, perhaps, David would return better than ever.

As I said earlier, my brother had made some sort of subconscious decision to become a man during the summer prior. Over the course of his rehabilitation, that decision became conscious and final. In addition to making a fervent comeback, David announced that his doctors had inspired him. He would become a doctor someday, and his academics soon garnered the same focused attention as did his athletics. He would maintain a 4.0 grade point average for the duration of high school. He wrote a paper on sports performance for his psychology class, it was shown to some college professors, and as it was of such high quality, it eventually helped him gain admission to Stanford University. (He made good on his promise and is currently regarded as one of the top anesthesiologists in Denver).

Another interesting development, another giant hurdle to David's return, had evolved in the Cherry Creek wrestling room. In David's absence, Jason Foster had dropped down to the 112-pound spot on the varsity and become an absolute terror. In anticipation of wrestling at 119 pounds, Jason had also adhered to an intense weight lifting program in the preseason (Coach Foster was a weight training fanatic). When he reversed direction and made the cut to 112 pounds, he was gargantuan for the weight class. Jason had long arms and his father/coach had adapted his takedowns to suit this advantage, employing a quick, "snag" style of single-leg takedown that didn't require hitting a knee. No one could stop it. Jason started out the season slowly, having a bit of trouble adjusting to the weight and new level of competition. But as time passed, he began giving top-ranked wrestlers all they could handle, including me. I began to have great difficulty scoring on the kid, and in the back of my mind at each practice, I wondered how my brother would make his way back on the team.

One of the aspects I enjoy most about wrestling is its unbridled egalitarianism. Coaches don't pick the team; there are no politics involved. You wrestle your way onto the team, no matter what. This style of tryout is called a "wrestle-off." If you beat the wrestlers in your weight class, you start; otherwise, take a seat — simple Darwinism. Imagine showing up to work one day and having to throw down with a new recruit in order to maintain your employment— that's a wrestle-off. It doesn't matter if the guy below you might fare better in competition, it doesn't matter if you get injured— you earn your way on the team, period. Thus, the standard assumption was that David, fresh back in the practice room, would be required to face Jason Foster mano a mano.

Coach Foster called the two of us and asked us to meet both him and Jason in a private practice— just the four of us— the day before second semester classes began on January 14. My brother and I both assumed the purpose of the meeting would be to engage in some sort of clandestine wrestle-off and that, should my brother lose, he would be spared the indignity in front of the team. Classy move by Coach Foster, we thought, but we were both nervous and scared, our competitive juices flowing. Instead, once we arrived the next day, Coach Foster asked my brother to drill some wrestling moves on both Jason and me. He then asked that my brother wrestle "half speed" against each of us. Finally, he asked Jason and me to wrestle full speed. Coach's face cringed. One thing was abundantly clear to all of us. Despite our hopes, my brother was an absolute shell of his former self. At that moment, Jason was clearly the superior wrestler. Then Coach Foster did something unfathomable, something I have never seen again in the sport of wrestling. He paused, as if the painful words needed time to emerge, then he told us that, as hard as it was for him as a coach and parent, Jason would cede the spot to my brother and return to 119 pounds on the JV. All of us were stunned, Jason included. Nevertheless, Jason said not a word, and he handled the decision with complete and utter grace. Like Abraham bringing Isaac to the mount, Coach Foster had sacrificed his own parental dreams and his son's aspirations out of respect for my brother. Deep down, I think Steve Foster considered us both like sons because of our unmitigated love of wrestling. Still though, coach and son's collective act was one of the nicest things anyone has ever done for us. I am eternally grateful.

David returned to competition on time, and the initial results were a complete disaster. Prior to his injury, David and I often intimidated opponents with our warm-up routine. We would drill high-level moves at breakneck speed, pace back and forth like crazy junkyard dogs, and sprint to the middle of the mat once our names were called. You get the picture— high school bravado to tenth degree. Now, in place of this routine, David gingerly hobbled on his crutches to the mat. Opponents took notice, and he was forced to pull out of his first tournament of the season after receiving a vicious beating from the number one-ranked wrestler at 112 pounds. David's leg attacks were slow as molasses, and he struggled with his timing and execution. The following week, David was unceremoniously pinned by a crosstown rival to whom he had never lost. A local sports reporter who covered high school sports and had taken an unnatural dislike to the rich kids from Cherry Creek gushingly described my brother as having been "riveted" to the wrestling mat and saw fit to make sure it was printed on page one of the next edition of his local rag— a cruel and unnecessary blow to an injured sixteen-year-old. In the following weeks, David amassed a small winning streak against lesser league opponents, but all of us worried that he would have great difficulty simply qualifying for the state tournament. I couldn't help but wonder if Coach Foster had regretted his decision. Both Jason and I had gotten the better of David in the room, and we all silently prayed that some sort of inspiration would come. It did.

My brother— smart guy if there ever was one— wrote Barry Davis a letter, the old-fashioned way we now refer to as "snail mail." I never saw the letter, but as David described it to me, the message briefly detailed his injury and difficulties in moving, and it asked if Barry had any advice. In a matter of days, the phone rang in the evening—my mom answered—and it was Barry Davis. He asked for David; I couldn't help but pick up the phone and listen. The conversation lasted about three minutes total; Barry obviously did all the talking—really fast talking. David and I took copious notes, hung up the phone, and immediately congregated to start the translation process. Like a wrestling Mozart, Barry had composed a strategic symphony for my brother. Somewhere in the hasty conversation, my brother and I had gleaned that Barry emphasized the importance of David's lost speed from the injury— David would need to change. At the verbal equivalent of lightspeed, Barry instructed David to focus on defense, and only when he really, truly needed the points, was he to attack his opponent by surprising him off (perhaps a millisecond before) the referee's starting whistle. In the days following, there was an immediate improvement in David's wrestling. This strategy was the baseball equivalent of utilizing the changeup—a pitcher may only have an 85 mph fastball, but it seems like 100 mph after a few loping changeups. David's prior style (the style I still employed) was pure fastballs, relying heavily on leg attacks that put tremendous pressure on his ankle. As part of this tactical change, my brother adopted a squared, defensive stance and developed an effective front headlock. It took him awhile to gain comfort, but I remember the exact practice when, as Barry instructed, David first lulled me to sleep and nailed me with a single-leg takedown off the whistle. It was the first time he had scored on me in the room since his comeback, and I knew things had turned. From time to time, he would cryptically refer to this new style as "Barry's secret strategy," and he declared privately to me that he would shock all doubters and medal in the state tournament.

In the following weeks preceding the state tournament, things progressed. David was required to beat several tough local wrestlers to qualify for state, and he lost in the district tournament to the same crosstown rival. Nevertheless, we were encouraged that David gave the kid a real run for his money this time. The brackets for the state tournament were printed the next day in the *Denver Post*, and our stomachs collectively dropped. David's weight class was absolutely loaded; several highly ranked wresters at 119 had dropped down because they feared Scott Gates. David was one of the few wrestlers with a "pigtail" match—an extra match in the preliminaries just to get into the thirty-two-man bracket.

David's first opponent was no slouch, a state qualifier at 119 pounds the year before. The match was incredibly tight, and it was tied with twenty seconds remaining. For the first time in competition, David employed his surprise attack at the referee's whistle (possibly a millisecond before) and scored a takedown just prior to the closing buzzer. We all felt as much relief as elation. At least David did not get put out the first round. The same night, David won a barn burner of a match, somehow gaining a reversal in the third period to win. In the third round, David faced the eventual state champion, a tough-as-nails kid from northern Colorado who smartly and mercilessly attacked David's ankle. The customized Aircast attached to David's leg literally exploded from being squeezed like a blood orange. Several times David screamed in pain, and he very nearly succumbed to an injury default. The match was an agonizing blowout, and it resembled many of David's early debacles. All of us wondered with apprehension how David would respond. He would need to win two straight matches to medal, and both opponents were darn good wrestlers. In his next match that night, my brother composed himself and beat a multiple-time state medalist in a smart, defensive win. One more to go tomorrow. His next opponent was a young prodigy, just hitting his prime. He would go on in later years to become an elite wrestler and earn multiple state championships, junior national medals, and a full ride to Minnesota— a tough challenge, to say the least.

After our final weigh-ins the next morning, our entire team headed back to the hotel to rest up and mentally prepare for the most important day of the season. I would be wrestling in the finals that night, along with Gates, but we had several wrestlers, my brother included, who were wrestling in the placing rounds that morning. In a decision that puzzled all of us, my brother decided to stay behind and spend the next three hours at the arena. David bypassed the security guard and passed the time soaking up the atmosphere, warming up in the giant facility alone, listening to echoes. After all the adversity, with possibly more to come, my brother decided he deserved a little fun. David showed up to matside almost too loose; his demeanor worried me, but it shouldn't have—he knew what he was doing. The match was a slugfest. Each wrestler traded several skilled takedowns, and my brother looked surprisingly athletic, as if reconjuring a bit of his October prowess. Nevertheless, my brother trailed by two points with forty-five seconds left, and things looked bleak. Out of nowhere, my brother executed a reversal called a "power switch," which I had never seem him utilize. Two points—the match was tied. At that point, all of us crossed our fingers that my brother could ride his opponent out and get a new life in overtime. Thirty seconds remained.

Instead, David intentionally and seemingly inexplicably conceded an escape point—with the clock burning down and as his opponent sprung to his feet, David stepped out-of-bounds for safety. David now trailed by one point with twenty seconds left. He chose to double down and attempt the takedown and win. Flashbacks of my brother's strategic snafu a year earlier reverberated in my mind; all of us cringed. We had all forgotten about "Barry's secret strategy," and like lightning, my brother shot a double-leg takedown right at (possibly a millisecond prior to) the whistle. His opponent was stunned and toppled to his back. Time expired—my brother had won. The next few seconds were blurry. There was my brother jumping in Coach Foster's arms and the crowd, recognizing the extent of David's injury and the magnitude of the accomplishment, cheering uncharacteristically loudly. My brother let out a primal scream, his arms in the air. And there was crying, lots of joyous, unrestrained, blissful crying. What a moment! David had won his first state medal, and despite losing his next two matches to outstanding wrestlers, he looked fantastic. I have never been prouder of any of our collective accomplishments than David's sixth-place state medal. Greatest state tournament ever, if you ask me.

As I expressed above, the moral to this story is that *how* we experience the journey of our endeavors far outweighs the importance of the actual results. The record books will reflect a muted sixth-place finish, but make no mistake, this was a personal, human, and spiritual championship of magnanimous proportions—one that will last us both a lifetime. The strength and habits my brother gained from rebuilding his shattered, teenage self have served him well and multiplied into many successes later down the road. I often wonder if, had he not broken his leg, had he easily won a state championship, would he be the same man? Probably—he's that good of a person—but you never know. Aristotle was correct: we are what we do.

PS—As a side note, if things get tough in your life, I would highly advise against the following: eating eleven birthday cakes, any type of velour sweat suit, French berets, or bad perms. Word to the wise.

Namaste.

STORY 6

BAD KARMA AND MOONPIES

*No matter what, if you do the right thing,
it will always work in your favor.*
— Phil Nowick, author

I'm not proud of this story, far from it. Nevertheless, my brother, who has thus far taken a merciless ribbing in the book, deserves vindication. As you peel back the layers of this story and get past the hilarity, it boils down to a young man acting deceitfully and running away from consequences, then ultimately finding the right path as such consequences catch up with him in a big way. As this story illustrates, I had developed a penchant— dare we say "talent"— in my youth for bending the rules. David and I were nineteen years old at the time; the year was 1989. We were sophomores in college, each of us competing at the 118-pound weight class. David had won a starting spot at Stanford University, which was known more for producing Nobel laureates than NCAA champion wrestlers. I still languished as a backup for the University of Michigan, a solid academic institution with an intense pride in athletic achievement, competing in the Big Ten Conference with wrestling juggernauts such as Iowa, Penn State, and Minnesota. The story unfolds on a brutally cold December weekend in Evanston, Illinois, in which David and I were each competing for our respective schools at the prestigious Midlands Wrestling Championship, held at Northwestern University. Despite our numerous adventures and debacles, we had existed on planet Earth for two decades without so much as a flirtatious attempt at the ultimate identical twin caper—the old switcheroo. Hard to believe, but each of us saw such behavior as the boundary line for human independence. We had met other sets of identical twins that dressed alike, talked alike, and quite often reveled in an opportunity that many people dream of: actually and credibly stepping into another's shoes without anyone noticing, if only for a moment. But the act, to us, seemed like trading in our distinctive identities for one amorphous existence.

David and I are a rare form of identical twins called "mirror image" twins, literally flip-flopped carbon copies of each other. I am left-handed; he is right-handed. I had a standard wrestling stance (right leg forward); my brother utilized a left leg lead, akin to a southpaw boxer. I kick a ball with my right foot, he the left. When we were eleven, our family orthodontist stared in disbelief at the newly formed plaster molds of our teeth. We had the exact same flaws in our dental structure, only on opposite sides of our mouths. If you believe in the concept, David was somewhat left-brained as a youth; he was responsible, a strong believer in rules and ethics, more linear in thought, and had migrated to organic chemistry and biology in his premed major (as I mentioned, he had decided at age sixteen to become a doctor). Conversely, I could have been perceived as more right-brained. I was less organized, less willing to accept convention, more big picture-focused, and chose business and economics as an academic pursuit. I had two additional right-brained traits that served me poorly that bitter cold weekend in December. First, I was superstitious, and I feared that switching identities with my brother, even for the briefest period of time, would anger the wrestling gods and result in immediate bad karma and retribution. Second, to put it lightly, I had a somewhat morally flexible view of the world, always looking for the loophole or shortcut to the standard or rule. My penchant for the latter overcame the former and, as you will read, predictably blew up in my face. The debacle at the Midlands Tournament would be my first of many lessons related to a premise that I have come to swear by: there are no shortcuts in life.

College wrestling had been a rude awakening to say the least. The flip side to making the choice to chase an endeavor to its logical end—be it a career, academics, or peripheral pursuits, such as sports, music, etc.—is the inevitable step up into the big pond. You might be the most talented chess player in your area, ruling the park benches in your neighborhood with impunity. You might be a journalistic prodigy for your school and local papers. But enter a national competitive chess tournament or attempt to publish your work as a freelance writer in nationally read publications, and you quickly realize that countless people exist with equal or more talent, sharper focus, and years more of experience. Over time, the choice is simple: improve your game dramatically or perish. Your commitment to the pursuit is immediately stress-tested and the crucible question is posed to you: are you willing to swallow a prolonged diet of failure to ultimately taste a morsel of success? The phrase "labor of love" must have been coined somewhere in this process. I did indeed love the sport of wrestling and, approaching the Midlands tournament, had feasted on two years' worth of countless such "learning experiences" in the form of having my nose ground into the maize and blue mats for the Michigan Wolverines. The Midlands tournament would serve as a low point in this development process.

My collegiate wrestling career actually started out with promise, believe it or not. Ah yes, bright, shiny promise that lasted all of twenty-four hours. Despite being one of the most highly regarded wrestlers in Colorado my senior year in high school, I was not exactly a blue-chip recruit. Colorado and the Rocky Mountain region had scant few college wrestling programs, thus my home state was generally regarded as a second- or third-tier wrestling area. College coaches in the wrestling-rich Midwest need not look beyond their own borders of Ohio, Iowa, Michigan, or Pennsylvania for talent. Absent a ski weekend or camping expedition, Colorado was likely not on the recruiting dance card. Thus, at the conclusion of high school, being armed with good grades, continued delusions of grandeur regarding my wrestling ability, and generous parents willing to foot my tuition, I enrolled at the University of Michigan and joined the wrestling team as a walk-on.

My first formal wrestling practice at Michigan occurred in late September. In my weight class, a total of three full-scholarship athletes—two seniors and another freshman (a three time Michigan state champion)—stood beside me as our coach addressed us for the first time that season. We would all be vying for a single spot on the team. Unlike me—the walk-on from Colorado—each of my competitors/ teammates was a much-heralded and highly recruited wrestler from the Midwest, where wrestling matters. We also had a graduate assistant coach for the lightweights—his name was Willie Water, and he had achieved All-American status the year prior as a senior and now stuck around to try his hand on the international circuit while coaching and earning a master's degree.

As the brief motivational speech concluded, I immediately realized that college practices would not be the collegial, team-oriented, mentoring experiences of my high school days, in which a good hour or more was dedicated to instruction and technical development. "Get a partner and battle for the next ninety minutes. Practice ends when one of you quits," our coach instructed in a deadpan voice. This form of practice was appropriately named a "grind" practice and was designed to test your mettle. I was paired up with one of the seniors and surprisingly held my own for the ensuing hour and a half. My takedowns worked well—no one in the room had seen me wrestle and I used that novelty to my advantage. I was able to push the pace—I had worked myself into top shape in preparation over the summer whereas my opponent's timing and conditioning were in early-season form. Jeers arose from the coaching staff at my opponent. "Don't let that freshman score on you like that!" Practice ended, and the head coach sauntered up to me and bluntly gave me what I think was supposed to be encouragement. "You're not half as bad as we thought you would be. You can actually wrestle. If you keep working, you're going to turn into an excellent practice partner for our guys on scholarship someday," he said, a sort of halfhearted attempt at being gracious. "Thanks, I think," I replied. Not exactly the motivational speech I was used to from Coach Foster back home.

As they say, the other shoe began to drop in our second practice the next day. I was paired up with our grad assistant coach, Willie Waters. Willie stood about 5'6" to my Lilliputian 5'1" and outweighed me by around ten pounds, which may not sound like much but in the sport of wrestling can present a tremendous advantage. Willie was twenty-four years old—having used the full five years of his eligibility (he had probably wrestled over 200 college matches during that time)—to my eighteen years. Willie had the build of a full-grown man—hard and wiry—compared to my athletic but still somewhat boyish build. Willie was African-American with panther-like quickness in contrast to my slow, plodding style emanating from my stocky, Eastern European genes. You get the picture; I was about to get my ass kicked.

We locked horns in another grind practice, and similar to the day prior, the workout started with potential. I was able to hold position and initially able to ward off Willie's first offensive forays (or so I thought). He appeared almost lax in his approaches, bobbing, moving, and feinting, occasionally shooting half a takedown but never really committing to anything. It was then that I realized the primary difference between high school and college wrestling. High school wrestlers come out with both guns blazing, oblivious of everything but their methods of attack. College wrestlers observe and diagnose, probing for weaknesses, looking to stick the knife in deep when an opening occurs—and Willie had found his opening.

I had a flaw in my stance, an error common to many high school wrestlers. It is a cardinal rule in wrestling that the lower your wrestling stance, the better. Willie had discovered that I had a fatal habit of standing straight up when my opponent snapped my head. He tested the premise gingerly at first, simply tapping my head and following with more fakes and movement. Minutes later, as Willie closed in for his next approach, I felt a crash on the back of my neck so hard my teeth rattled and the rest seemed to disappear into a time warp. It was Willie's patented "blast double-leg" takedown, quick as lightning, in which he would snap my head, drop out of sight, and explode forward, his forehead colliding violently with my chest and ribs while he attacked both my legs at the knee. For the remainder of the workout, Willie proceeded to execute this technique over and over, as if he were putting on a blast double-leg clinic for the rest of the room, often knocking me from a standing position straight to my back.

I would learn the second major difference between a college and high school wrestling room over the duration of my freshman year. It would be a constant affirmation of a sad but inalienable rule of big-time college athletics—"Every Man for Himself," a pervasive attitude that extended to both your teammates and, unfortunately, coaches. "Full-ride" scholarships are not what they seem to the average college sports fan. A common belief for many is that an athletic scholarship is a four- sometimes five-year commitment to the "student athlete" to cover tuition, books, and expenses, etc., that no matter what, once an athlete signs on the dotted line, his coaches have chosen "their guy" for that time period and will stick with him through thick and thin. Not so. Generally speaking, an athletic scholarship has a fine-print clause that states that it will be renewed annually at the coaching staff's leisure, which means that an athlete can have the rug pulled out from under him somewhat hastily if he does not perform.

Thus, if you take the technical flaw I had in my stance as an example, an older and more experienced teammate in a high school room might point the problem out, and it is a strong bet that your high school coach would make it his charge in life to teach and drill you endlessly until the problem was fixed. This mentoring process rarely exists in a college room. Your teammates at your weight class and the surrounding weights aren't about to give up such a precious advantage as they put their scholarships on the line every day. Head coaches have livelihoods to protect as well and can far more easily replace you with a bright, shiny blue-chip recruit than they can spend countless hours cultivating your skills until you reach your potential.

"What about the grad assistants, such as Willie, who are a mix of teammate and coach as they actually work out with you in the room?" you ask. Surely they have no conflict of interest. Yes and no. Any wrestler good enough to secure such a grad assistant position did so by being intensely competitive, and it is unlikely this trait will change as he transitions in his role. Additionally, grad assistants also learned via the school of hard knocks during their competitive tenures and likely took the grad assistant position *specifically to inflict similar lessons on future generations of wrestlers.* Finally, grad assistants don't last too long if they get beat in the room. Thus, despite being one of the nicest guys I have ever met, Willie was not about to release such an advantage, at least not right away. Eventually, an entire year later during a summer workout, Willie confided in me that all of the lightweights in the Michigan room had learned to snap my head and shoot from the outside. The problem took all of fifteen minutes to fix, and I finally learned to defend myself against an outside attack.

I digress—back to my second college practice, also known as the "worst butt-kicking in the history of my wrestling." I learned many things about myself and about the sport in the ensuing ninety minutes. I learned that my voice could reach soprano levels that had previously been untested as Willie saw fit to execute not just pinning combinations, but submission holds as well. I learned that if the room is hot enough, with a proper amount of sweat finding its way to the mats on the floor, and if you are thrown high enough and land hard enough, it is possible to produce both a visible and audible splash. Lastly, I learned that I had much to learn, and my status immediately returned from potential surprise to lowly, nonexistent, walk-on in the Michigan wrestling room.

Suffice it to say, the learning process necessary to develop into a passable college wrestler doesn't happen overnight. In truth, the transition, even for a highly touted high school recruit, can be painful. The leap seemed doubly hard for me—and for my brother, halfway across the US at Stanford—for several reasons. First, we were, in fact, not used to facing the high level of competition in Colorado that recruits from Oklahoma, Ohio, or Pennsylvania faced on a regular basis. Once you step into a college room, you face an all-star team of wrestlers from all over the country, every day. Second, both David and I had somewhat unevenly rounded skill sets at that point—strong on leg attacks, glaring weaknesses in the areas of mat wrestling and defense. The first step to becoming a decent college wrestler is developing good defense. As high school wrestlers, we rarely needed to defend anything; no one could stop our leg attacks, "So why bother learning defense?" we reasoned. Third, it would take a couple of years for us to mature physically into the 118-pound weight class, if you can believe that. We wrestled at 112 pounds and 105 pounds, respectively, in high school, and we both had normal weights around 123 pounds. A decent-sized 118-pounder walks around at about 130 pounds in the summer. The physical difference between a twenty-three-year-old fifth year senior and an eighteen-year-old freshman can be borderline comical, and it often was in our case—I would marvel at the giant legs, full-grown beards, ripped muscles, and tattoos of some of my opponents.

Finally, if we stick with our "little-fish-big-pond" analogy, college wrestling is like jumping into the shark-infested waters of the freaking

Atlantic Ocean compared to anything you could experience in high school. No matter where you are from, if you can hold your own on a college wrestling mat, you are a pretty damn good wrestler. The difference between the starter for Ohio State and the starter for Cuyuhoga State Community College is often that the latter is an outstanding wrestler with crappy grades, but they don't give you points for knowing calculus at a college wrestling tournament. So you learn not to judge a book by its cover; everybody can roll in college. Long story short, we took a healthy dose of beatings, both at practices and in competitive matches, our first two years in college. Most people would have quit after such a prolonged period of frustration, but we had an advantage. We loved the sport, loved it with all of our hearts, even if it didn't love us back at the time.

I am convinced that the above tests of athletic perseverance pale in comparison, however, to the greatest challenge and most daunting hurdle to making it as a college wrestler: fun. That's right, fun, as in any activity that provides instant amusement and enjoyment. Fun is the kryptonite to the blind commitment and discipline required to become an elite-level wrestler or fighter. The sport of wrestling is demanding, grueling, and brutally challenging from physical, mental, and cognitive standpoints—the antithesis of fun. Don't get me wrong, the adrenaline rush and sense of reward that you experience in defeating a top-level opponent in the sport of wrestling is absolutely unmatched in terms of pure human gratification, but the concept of fun does not compute in wrestling.

For those of us lucky enough to have the talent and physical/mental makeup to last through our 4–5 years of college wrestling (perhaps longer if you choose to compete on the Olympic circuit), careers end one of three ways: First, a wrestler's body gives out. It could be a blown knee ligament or shoulder tear or simply age, which robs a wrestler of his split-second reflexes. Second, a wrestler's mind grows weary of the sport and longs for simple pleasures he so often denied himself. He gets tired of skipping Thanksgiving dinner, eating carrots and celery with diet ranch dressing like an idiot at the kiddies' table. He grows weary of falling asleep in class or at work because he got up at 6:00 a.m. to get in the necessary cardio or running exercise. He wonders what it would be like to sleep in, just once, until 9:00 a.m. and have a clear head and the proper amount of rest during the day. He decides that doing things like maintaining a body fat percentage below 7 percent, or drilling wrestling techniques until the mind numbs, or dehydrating your body to the point of medical emergency in order to make weight is ridiculous behavior, whereas such actions seemed completely rational just a day before. Finally, a wrestling career ends because life simply takes over. One cannot exist in the modern world as a spartan warrior forever. So a wrestler takes a summer internship to bolster his résumé instead of training at camps with his team. He meets a girlfriend, and a sense of softness and compassion enters his life—death to a fighter. He begins to move on. As I stated above, fun, in large enough doses, tends to act as a catalyst in this last case, accelerating the end.

On that point, college life, especially at a large, storied, athletics-crazy institution such as the University of Michigan, has more than its fair share of pure, unadulterated fun. Outside of the columns of serious buildings like the library, business school, or law school, the remaining infrastructure of Ann Arbor, Michigan, is geared solely around the industry of college fun—T-shirt shops sporting entire wardrobes of the maize and blue team colors, countless pizza and sandwich parlors open until 2:00 a.m., a long line of fraternity and sorority houses, and numerous establishments that form the staple of any college town economy: college bars. The most important ingredient, however, is female coeds as far as the eye can see. On weekends in the fall, during football season, an endless procession of Winnebago trailers and campers head to Ann Arbor from all directions, beginning Thursday afternoon until game time on Saturday. Thousands of dedicated fans for both the home and away teams land in the parking lot of Michigan Stadium to root for their beloved alma maters. The campus is transformed into a giant outdoor festival, replete with pep rallies, cheerleaders, grilled bratwursts, and oceans of beer from kegs consumed in red plastic cups. Fun oozes out of the atmosphere.

I arrived in Ann Arbor with the rest of the bright-eyed and bushy tailed college freshmen in late August. My mom flew out with me from Denver, having packed every conceivable necessity that would fit into a college dorm room. I knew that I would be staying in South Quad, where many of the athletes resided. My roommate would be a heavyweight on our wrestling team, also an incoming freshman, also named Phil—Phil Tomek. My mom and I drove in our rental car down State Street on a gorgeous afternoon. In every direction, mothers and fathers alike all sweated through the sunny but slightly muggy autumn weather, unloading bedding, clothing, and care packages, determined to send their now-grown babies off in proper fashion.

I had spoken to Phil Tomek (we will call him "Big Phil" for reasons I outline below) one time on the phone a week prior as I was packing for the trip at our home in Denver. We planned out the logistics of the dorm room, each praying the other would not be some sort of loony (as it turned out, we would both turn into nocturnal, unrestrained, pizza-eating barbarians by the school year's end, as do all college freshmen, so our fears were unwarranted). The conversation was awkward, polite, and civil, the last of such conversations I would ever have with Big Phil. We discussed what we'd each bring to the room: I had a microwave, he had a VCR, I had a giant Swatch watch that functioned as a working clock to hang on the wall (it was the eighties, cut me a break), he had a poster of our favorite US Olympic wrestler, Dave Schultz, and so on.

Big Phil was a super blue-chip recruit because he possessed two incredibly rare traits highly sought-after by college coaches. First and foremost, he was a big, huge lunk of a young man. Not fat at all, tall—well over six feet—lanky, thick, with hands like meat cleavers. Ninety-nine percent of the athletes his size had opted for football, but not Big Phil. His father, George Tomek, was first-generation Czechoslovakian, and he was an absolute fanatic about two sports, soccer and wrestling, both of which Big Phil excelled at from early youth to high school graduation. Second, Phil had incredibly light feet for an athlete his size, likely from the years of soccer, and he possessed a wrestling style more akin to a 134-pounder than a plodding heavyweight. Big Phil was also well-schooled with impeccable wrestling technique. Rather than take the underwhelming scholarship offers he had out of high school as a possible 177- or 190-pounder, Big Phil chose to take an entire year off prior to enrolling in college to train at Northwestern University with Olympians Jim and Bill Scherr. This required Big Phil to take a two-hour ride every day on the L Train each way from his home in Wheaton, Illinois, to Evanston. The work paid off. Big Phil grew into his frame and developed into a rare and valuable wrestling commodity: a heavyweight that could move.

The Michigan coaches were thrilled to land Big Phil. As they say, however, careful what you wish for—they were in for quite a ride. I say this in jest because Big Phil would spend the next five years specializing in driving the Michigan coaches crazy—a pursuit that brought him infinite joy. In so many facets of life, Big Phil was wonderfully unpredictable. On a personal level, he could best be described as joyously erratic, as he reveled in finding delight, amusement, and humor in every situation. One could simply marvel at what this gentle giant of a man would do from one moment to the next. Whatever path of action he chose, his actions were, without fail, hilarious, whether he meant them to be or not.

Big Phil's approach to wrestling was equally capricious. His matches had a volatile ebb and flow, like a Greek tragedy in which Big Phil was the athletic protagonist—full of promise and power—with the inevitable Achilles' heel. At some point in the contest, he would display athleticism, technique, and footwork that convinced you he was destined for greatness, only to oftentimes shoot himself in the foot with confounding lapses in concentration. Big Phil was just as likely to handily beat the top-ranked wrestler in the nation at his weight class (which he did many times) as he was to lose to an absolute journeyman. Big Phil's wrestling career was solid and successful, certainly beyond what I would have hoped to achieve—he qualified for the NCAAs numerous times, and he achieved all-American status in 1991. And there were a few moments when he was the best upper-weight wrestler I ever saw in college. It always made you wonder what went wrong when he'd lose what you'd think would have been any easy match. In any case, I knew the moment my mom and I walked into that dorm room in South Quad—Big Phil's giant legs stretching past the capacity of the hopelessly inadequate twin bed—that we would be great friends.

We took an hour or so to unpack. My mom, who stands about 4'10", was simply awestruck by Big Phil's giant features. I took a few moments in the hall to say my goodbyes, and I manifested a superhuman effort not to join my mom in a good cry; I didn't want my new roommate to think I was a pansy. I reentered the room, and Big Phil immediately wanted to take care of the first order of business as roommates. It would be too awkward and confusing for both of us to have the same name, Phil. He declared from that point on that he would answer to the moniker "Big Phil" and I would be aptly named "Little Phil." I groused at the suggestion, but who was I to argue—the kid outweighed me by one hundred pounds. Second, he stated, "Your mom's gone; we need to loosen you up. Let's grab something to eat and go to Dooley's." Big Phil had attended summer school in Ann Arbor and worked at the University of Michigan Wrestling Camps. He knew all of the guys on the wrestling team, which featured several returning all-Americans, and he had become a connoisseur of all things fantastic on the Michigan campus. South Quad had a festive air to it, one that never seemed to go away, and we headed down State Street to a somewhat famous lunch dive called Mister Spots for sandwiches and waffle fries smothered in cheese. As the meal wound down, I asked what type of establishment Dooley's was. "It's an awesome bar; you get in free if you're an athlete and you don't have to wait in line," Big Phil told me. I gave him a confused look. Both of us were below the legal drinking age—how would we get in? I inquired. Big Phil laughed openly—how could I be so naïve ...

And so it began. The rest of the week was amazing. Classes did not begin for a few days, and we imbibed late into the night at Dooley's, ate amazing pizza from Cottage Inn, and enjoyed my favorite aspect of campus life: girls, girls, girls. I had never met so many girls in my life. Don't get me wrong—in high school, I did okay with getting dates. But college was different. All of us were free from the caste system imposed upon us in our much smaller high schools, and we had the chance to reinvent ourselves. Thus, I would become "Little Phil"—college wrestler, somewhat serious student, lover of pizza and waffle fries, and world-class girl-chaser. Man, we had fun. The entire experience was a blur and, without question, one of the craziest and most enjoyable times of my life.

Flash forward a year and a half. The honeymoon was over. I was knee-deep into my major classes—economics, accounting, statistics ... no soft touch at Michigan. I had toughened up a bit in the Michigan wrestling room, but I certainly hadn't made any quantum leaps in the sport. I had a .500 record in my matches at the preseason tournaments and had lost my "challenge" matches to obtain the varsity spot at 118 pounds by a reasonably close margin. My coaches told me that, if I performed well at the Midlands, which was a highly prestigious tournament with not only the top-ranked college wrestlers but also several former NCAA all-Americans and champions, then I would receive another challenge match to make the team when we returned to school. If I did not win the challenge match, that was it—I would have to wait another year for a chance to make the team. I had added about seven pounds to my frame, most of it good weight, and I walked around at about 125 pounds. As it is held over Christmas break, the Midlands gave a generous allowance of four pounds from my division's "scratch" weight (the weight you had to make at the NCAAs) of 118 pounds, so I would have to weigh in at 122 pounds. I knew from vast past experiences that I would easily be able to sweat off the three pounds with a good workout lasting about ninety minutes—sixty minutes if I had my plastic "sauna suit."

The Michigan coaches were candid and open that they were using this tournament as a final measuring stick for both me—the walk-on from Colorado who insisted on missing practices for petty things like review sessions for final exams—and the holder at the time of the varsity spot—a much-heralded three-time state champ with a full scholarship who also had scantly above a .500 wrestling match record. If neither of us impressed, they would move on and recruit several of the top high school lightweights. "No pressure though, we are in your corner … we believe in you … unless … well, you know … whatever," was the best motivational speech our coaches could conjure. Somehow I did not feel reassured.

As with most of my bigger mistakes in life, the Midlands debacle was self-inflicted. My first error in judgment was to accept an invitation to Big Phil's home in Wheaton, Illinois, to spend some time with his family and, in theory, make the trip to Evanston shorter. Big Phil and I had become thick as thieves at that point. I was the little brother he never had. Big Phil had no reservations, for instance, about picking me up like a five-foot ragdoll and swinging me by my ankles if the impulse so struck him. Also, it wasn't uncommon for him to bust into our dorm room or my campus apartment the next year and demonstrate the efficacy of the latest choke hold or high-amplitude foot sweep he had learned, without so much as a greeting. Big Phil had also changed my name. About midway through our freshmen year, I told him that I didn't want to be called "Little Phil" anymore. The name didn't suit me. He gave me a contemplative look, put a few moments of thought into the matter, and declared, "Okay. We'll call you the Oompa-Loompa. You know, like those little orange midgets in *Willy Wonka*; you remind me of one of those." I laughed, as I always did, at his deadpan humor, because I thought he was joking. Not so. Big Phil was stone-cold serious, and the name caught on like wildfire. My teammates on the Michigan wrestling team went crazy at the notion, and I was never known as Phil Nowick again on the Michigan campus. Big Phil would have random girls approach me at Dooley's and ask, "Are you the Oompa-Loompa? What is Willy Wonka's factory like?" Other times he would instruct beautiful coeds on campus to run up to me singing the OompaLoompa song: "Oompa-Loompa Doopidy Doo!" My skin crawls just thinking about the theme. When David came out to work at the University of Michigan Wrestling Camps with me in the summer, everyone decided to shorten and differentiate the name. I was "Oompa," and David was "Loompa."

As Big Phil and his father, George, picked me up at Chicago O'Hare International Airport on a bitterly cold late December afternoon, Big Phil bellowed out, his hands cupped, "Oompa-Loompa!" Even the busy travelers passing by seemed to get the joke and snickered. George Tomek did not understand—he owned and ran his own tool and dye manufacturing business in Chicago and had no knowledge of Willy Wonka (although they very likely could have exchanged ideas about manufacturing processes). "Why do you call Little Phil the Oompa?" George asked in his thick Czech accent. Big Phil explained it to him, and his dad exploded with old-world European laughter. I would transfer to Stanford University after my sophomore year for many reasons,but not lost among those reasons was my desire to escape the dreaded nickname Oompa-Loompa. That particular story was just the beginning of the end.

I say it was a mistake to stay with the Tomeks for the days preceding the Midlands tournament because their hospitality was far too good. Like Big Phil, the Tomeks were a kind, jovial, wonderful family: Big Phil's older brother (who wrestled in college at Northwestern) and two sisters (also star athletes), his dad (already mentioned), and his mom, who lavished food and drink upon her tiny guest. Likely because of the Christmas holiday, it seemed there was a reason to celebrate with some type of food at every juncture of the day . They insisted I had never eaten pizza until I tried deep-dish Pizzeria Uno. They insisted I had never had a real hot dog until I tried a Chicago bratwurst. The entire family was close to six feet or taller. The men in the Tomek family were all more than twice my size, so clearly we viewed portion size a tad differently at meals. I am convinced the Tomek men could have been a traveling band of world-champion competitive eaters if they so chose, and they demonstrated such prowess at every meal.

Unlike the rest of our starters on the wrestling team, who often lost up to twenty pounds from their summer training weight in order to make their weight class, Big Phil labored to gain enough weight to hang with the big boys at heavyweight. Thus, eating became an Olympic sport for Big Phil. I grew a bit nervous as the belt line on my jeans began to feel tighter. I asked if the family had a scale in the house; they laughed. "We're trying to fatten you up, so we can have barbecued Oompa-Loompa," Big Phil quipped at the dinner table. This was standard conversation between us by then. "Yes!" George bellowed in his thick accent. "We will eat the Oompa!" The entire family now cackled uncontrollably, and I was more than a little afraid. As it turned out, I put on about three pounds during my two-day stay—not a huge deal, but it would require me to have a pretty long, sweaty weight-cutting session a few hours before weigh-ins. In any case, I wasn't worried; I usually made the weight easily.

As it turned out, the problem would not be one of weight, but of time and temperature. The Tomeks located a bathroom scale, which read that I weighed 127.5 pounds, a new record for me. The original plan was for George to drive us from Wheaton to Evanston, but an emergency came up at the tool and dye plant and the family was short a car. "No problem, we can catch the L Train. We'll make it in plenty of time," Big Phil exclaimed. I explained that I would probably need to arrive three hours prior to weigh-ins to ensure enough time to lose the weight. He seemed confident we would make it in time, so I didn't worry. It would actually feel good to sweat some of the rich food out of my system, I thought.

Periodically, a friend might ask in casual conversation, "What's the coldest you've ever been?" I have no problem recollecting that question: it was that morning. If you hail from the edges of the country and have somehow never ventured to Illinois in winter, there are two types of cold in the US: cold and Chicago cold. Mother Nature gave us ample demonstration that morning as to why Chicago is called the "Windy City." The temperature was five degrees Fahrenheit, but the raging winds easily made it feel like it was twenty degrees below zero. Along with my workout bag, replete with two thick pairs of sweats, my plastic sauna suit, running shoes, etc., I toted a massive duffel bag of household items, a Nintendo gaming system, other holiday gifts, clothing, and other random stuff that I had accumulated in Denver over the Christmas break. The duffle bag easily weighed over one hundred pounds and was beyond cumbersome.

As Mr. Tomek dropped us off at the train station, the cold hit me like a Mike Tyson left hook as soon as we got out of the car. Big Phil was bundled efficiently, with long underwear, a goose-down winter coat, a hat with earflaps, and double-lined winter gloves. The same goes for the rest of the Chicagoans at the station. The idiot from Denver (me) on the other hand, wore a hooded sweatshirt with jeans and a stylish but inadequate leather coat. The cold penetrated the gaps of my outfit immediately, and I struggled mightily under the weight and unwieldy nature of my duffel bag. I was completely exhausted by the time we reached the train platform; my ears, hands, and feet had turned to stone. The journey to Evanston was an exercise in misery. We transfered several times from one train to another, and I stumbled comically like a drunken Sherpa under the weight of my pack. Midway through the trip, on our third connection, I lost Big Phil. I simply could not keep up with his lumbering strides through the crowd. Big Phil had a tendency to become lost in his own world, whistling and laughing to himself, and at some point, I think he simply spaced out that we were travelling together. He had taken the trip hundreds of times, and his brain had switched to autopilot. So we lost a good forty-five minutes trying to locate each other—forty-five minutes that I dearly needed.

We arrived at the Northwestern University gym in Evanston at 4:45 p.m. Weigh-ins would begin at 5:00 p.m. and would end promptly at 6:00 p.m. I was totally spent, physically and mentally, from the trip, and I was staring down one of the most intense workouts of my life with no time to rest. I had about an hour to sweat off a little more than five pounds. I sprinted to the locker rooms and changed into my weight-cutting gear: plastic sauna suit on first, next to the skin, then the two pairs of sweats.

My first challenge was to get my body temperature high enough to break a sweat; I had spent the last three hours frozen stiff. The Northwestern gym was cold, and no exercise equipment had been set out or wrestling mats unrolled, as is common courtesy for the hosts of a wrestling tournament to do before weigh-ins. I didn't even have a jump rope; I had forgotten mine at home. Hence, I was relegated to running up and down bleachers for the next hour. At my normal rate, working out fairly hard in a warm room, I could lose three pounds of water weight per hour fully hydrated. Every wrestler knows this fact about his body, how much weight you can sweat off in a given amount of time. I was certainly not depleted and once the frostbite wore off, I broke a raging sweat. It would simply be a race against the clock. Could I get my sweat glands to work on overdrive and lose the weight in time? I literally sprinted up and down those bleacher stairs for the next sixty minutes. My calves still throb to this day just thinking about that workout.

I did not stop exercising until 5:45 p.m., and by that time my coaches and teammates had begun looking for me. My entire team at Michigan had made weight and was foaming at the mouth to hop on the bus and eat dinner. Some of these athletes had dropped enormous amounts of weight that day—their faces were sunken in like the grim reaper's, and they could not believe that the 118-pounder who rarely cut a pound was now standing between them and the nearest all-you-can-eat buffet. My coaches were none too pleased either; I was not a popular guy among the Michigan Wolverines at that moment.

As I stripped down and presented my weigh-in card to the official, I spotted my brother at the other end of the gym. He had arrived separately with the Stanford team and had just stepped on the scale successfully. He no doubt was headed toward his workout bag, ready to kill a thirty-two-ounce Gatorade. I was not feeling confident as I neared the front of the weigh-in line. I had never lost anything close to five pounds in less than an hour. I knew that if I missed the weight that the Michigan coaches would simply wash their hands of me. I was a walk-on. I had a .500 record. I asked too many questions on the rare occasion they demonstrated a new wrestling technique. I had missed *two* practices that semester for some idiotic events called "review sessions" for my final exams in economics and accounting. I had lost my challenge matches. Why bother with this kid if he can't even make weight at a Christmas tournament?

I handed my weigh-in card to the official and he stared at me incredulously. "You already weighed in!" he proclaimed. I pointed to my brother and explained that we were twins. He laughed in exasperation and told me to step on the scale. In any case, he was unnecessarily put on notice that I had a twin brother—not good. I closed my eyes and stepped up. "Nope!" I heard the official say. "Half a pound over!" My coaches screamed with frustration. "For Christ's sake, Nowick, you're holding us up!" Apparently they too were more concerned with the upcoming meal at Ponderosa Steakhouse than the fact that one of their athletes might not be able to compete. "Get your goddamn sweats back on and run that weight off." I did the math in my head—I had ten minutes. I had lost my sweat. I had half a pound to lose. No way. I turned my gaze to my brother and percolated an evil, irresponsible thought. I had no other choice; it was time to resort to the switcheroo. Although I always knew it would bring me bad karma, I would have to convince David to weigh in for me.

I saw him in the bleachers digging through his bag for the precious bottle of Gatorade. My brother was five pounds bigger than I, and he had been the model of discipline over the Christmas break in order to make weight. He banished all offers of potato latkes and Chanukah cookies at our family's Jewish holiday celebration, and he worked out twice a day while I was living it up at the Tomeks'. He was clearly depleted and very much looking forward to banishing the desperate pain of dehydration that every wrestler comes to know and despise. He looked up and saw me.

"Hey, how was the ..." he attempted to say in greeting.

"Don't drink anything!" I blurted in a half whisper half shout, interrupting him.

"Why?" He paused and looked at me. In our secret twin language, he observed me and knew what I was thinking. "No. No way! Whatever you are thinking, I am not doing it! How in the hell did you not make weight?" he asked incredulously.

"We were late getting here!" I said. "Look, I don't have time to explain. Just put my sweats on, grab my weigh-in card, and step on the scale. No one will ever know."

"You're crazy, man. We could get in so much trouble!" There was a sense of worry in his voice because, in the depths of his mind, he knew he would do most anything for me.

"You owe me, man!" To this day I still cringe at the guilt trip I was laying on him. "Who do you think cut all that weight in high school for four years so you could be at the right weight class?" It was true; I made it a standard practice of losing up to twenty pounds from a very healthy weight of 120 to 125 to make the 98 and 105-pound weight classes in high school. When you have a twin brother on your team, one of two things happens. You cut ridiculous amounts of weight and land in a weight class too low, or he moves up and gets pushed around. We chose the former path, although my true motivation was blind ambition. I wanted a high school state championship in the worst way and would have cut the weight regardless … most likely. My brother, who is a kind soul, certainly felt his share of my pain watching the things I had to do to myself to make the weight. It wasn't like he was fat and happy—he had lost a great deal of weight as well, but I had crossed the line of sanity, partially on his behalf.

"No way, man, not gonna happen," he said. He hadn't cracked yet, but I could tell by the tone of his voice he was wavering.

I paused. I couldn't think of what else to say that might convince him. I had already hit way, way below the belt. My brother, in a heartbeat, would have moved up in weight and taken on bigger opponents the moment I asked back in high school. He cared about me and wanted me to succeed. I knew that. But I pressed on. Like I said, my brother matured into a young man years before me. I was still playing the part of the little boy that didn't want to face the consequences of his own actions. Out of the depths of my mind, my retort burst forth, *"I gave you my MoonPie!"*

"What?" he beseeched. "What in the hell are you talking about? That was in junior high!"

Yes. The act of grace that I was speaking of took place in junior high. Long story short, we were thirteen years old and headed to Salina, Kansas, for the youth nationals in Coach Hendershot's red, seventies Dodge van. It was the first time David and I competed out of state and my first national level tournament victory at eighty-five pounds. Halfway there, our young stomachs grumbling, we stopped off in Burlington, Colorado, at a road stop and stocked up on candy and treats for after weigh-ins. I agonized over my choice and ultimately rolled the dice, jettisoning a vast array of Hostess treats for a confection called a MoonPie. I had never seen anything like it in my life, but with a name like MoonPie, how could you go wrong? So elated at my choice of treat was I, that I actually doubled down and purchased two MoonPies—one for after weigh-ins and one as a celebratory or consolation gift for myself, after I won or lost the tournament (I had all the bases covered).

For those of you not familiar with a MoonPie, it is a sandwich-like dessert treat that could best be described as chocolate-covered chaos. The ingredients don't have a lot of rhyme or reason: graham-crackery, cookie-like crusts with a marshmallow-like substance in the middle, all dipped in a chocolate armor. Like fine wine, it tastes best after having aged 2–3 years on a road stop or gas station shelf. Our teammate Chris Hendershot and his older brother, Kelly, chided me mercilessly the entire rest of the trip, making fun of my MoonPies. "MoonPie! MoonPie! Phil got a MoonPie! Hey, Phil! Can I have a bite of your *MoonPie*!" David chimed in without restraint, laughing hysterically. Already in a bad mood from my empty stomach and the long car ride, I fumed with rage.

Hours later, David's tune had changed. I found him weeping like an infant after weigh-ins. Some soulless scoundrel had stolen his candy and treats excellent choices, a Snickers and a package of Nutter Butter cookies. He had nothing to pacify his hunger, and he sat Indian-style in the bleachers wailing like a banshee. I decided to seize upon the opportunity and get right up in his face to taunt him as I reveled in MoonPie bliss, but—inexplicably—a bizarre feeling overcame me. I felt this strange, guilty sensation that I could not describe. I would later learn the feeling was called "compassion" or "sympathy," but to that point in my life I had felt none of it for my brother. As if an angel had somehow possessed my body, I forgot his open and wanton torment of my choice of treat during the trip and offered him my second MoonPie. It was a precious moment between us that only twins could experience, a memory that I now chose to sully by using it as emotional blackmail. But it did the trick.

"What do you want me to do?" he asked. I outlined the plan.

The time was 5:55 p.m.; we had little time to spare. I instructed David to follow me to the locker room. We entered adjacent bathroom stalls and switched clothing: I changed into his dry, clean jeans and Stanford hooded sweatshirt, while he changed into my wet, putrid sauna suit and two pairs of sweats. I gave him my weigh-in card and told him to wet his head in the sink to keep up the image of someone that miraculously found a way to lose half a pound in less than ten minutes. I would stay in the bathroom and remain in the stall. When the deed was done, he would return and we would switch clothes again. He left the bathroom alone, scared out of his mind to go step on the scale for his brother.

So there I stood, hiding in a bathroom stall, hiding from everything: my coaches, my teammates, and my own choices. I was at a low point in my life, and I knew it. I had dragged my brother into a ridiculous situation that likely could have cost both of us dearly had we been found out. For really the first time in my life, I knew I could blame the circumstances: the Tomeks' wonderful cuisine (I didn't want be a bad houseguest, did I?), the cold gym, the snafus on our trip, etc. But I knew the truth was that I simply didn't train and eat right like I should have, like David had. This extended to my wrestling and academic career as well. My grades were good but not great, my wrestling had improved, but marginally, and I blamed each on the other. The truth, however, was that I had allocated much of my time to living the good life in college and could have done a better job at both without sacrificing that much, like my brother had. Somehow I knew that, even if this little bamboozlement worked out—I was due for some bad karma. And I was.

I was awakened from my deep reflection by a loud knock on the stall door. "Dave, are you in there?" the voiced asked. Somehow I knew instinctively to answer as my brother. I opened the door to find a kid, about my age, with brown hair and comically large ears. He was wearing a cardinal-red Stanford University hooded sweatshirt. Although I hadn't met any of the Stanford wrestlers yet, I knew this was one of David's teammates—his name was Dave Sacks, a 134-pounder. We called him "Scrappy" because of his never-say-die attitude on the mat and his resemblance to the large-eared cartoon character Scrappy-Doo. He would turn out to be a great friend to both of us through the years.

I played along. "Yeah, um, yeah," was all I could think of to say.

"What the hell, dude?" Scrappy said. "Are you okay? The gym is almost empty. We've been looking for you. Your brother barely made it. His coaches were pissed man!"

"Where is he, do you know?" I asked.

"He got on the bus with his team, I assume. Come on, let's get out of here. We're all starving!" he said. I winced and realized that, at least for the time being, I was trapped in an alternative reality. I had become my brother David and would dutifully have to play that role until we were somehow reunited. Several problems existed: I had a vague recollection of the hotel at which we were supposed to stay, but no real idea where my brother was. Also, as we approached the Stanford coach and five Stanford wrestlers that were attending the tournament, I realized I knew none of these people. Luckily, I was able to recognize David's duffel bag—identical to mine but in a different color—and I picked it up off the bleachers and followed the rest of the Stanford crew.

We packed into a rented van and arrived at our hotel on the outskirts of Evanston. As we checked in, I had a moment of confusion when I reached inside my brother's jeans and found my brother's wallet, but I recovered and realized that, for that moment, I was Dave, and I gave the cashier his (or my) identification. I would be sharing a room with Scrappy, and we laid down our bags. As we headed out of the room to meet everybody in the lobby for dinner, Scrappy looked at me quizzically. "Aren't you going to bring your books, dude?"

"Books, what for?" I asked.

"You just spent the entire ride over here yammering how you were going to get a jump on your organic chemistry stuff. Plus, the rest of us are probably going to study for awhile after dinner, so …"

I interrupted him, "Oh yeah, yeah … I'm bringing my books."

"You're acting weird, man. I think that weight-cutting got to your blood sugar. Let's go to dinner," he said.

"I'm fine, dude. Let's go," I said, and I scrambled for what looked like David's backpack full of books. It was then that I realized how different David's and my first two years of college had been to that point. We continued to be mirror image twins. I felt quite comfortable in the classroom at Michigan, a highly reputable school, but I quickly realized that I needed to paddle hard to keep my head above water in the wresting room full of elite athletes. Conversely, my brother had easily made the starting spot on the Stanford wrestling team, but from an academic standpoint, Stanford was the big leagues, and he had to study harder than he ever imagined if he wanted to survive in classrooms full of valedictorians. For the Stanford wrestlers, this meant that they read most of their academic texts at home on Christmas break *before* classes had even started and that, if they had two hours of spare time after dinner at a wrestling tournament, they spent it studying.

The team had selected Denny's as the dinner spot because it was cheap and also because they served coffee late and would allow the team to study. Of the people I sat down with, the only names I knew were that of the coach, who had recruited both of us in high school, and Scrappy. I tried to say as little as possible as we ordered. The difference in demeanor between the Stanford and Michigan wrestlers was night and day. The Michigan wrestlers were warriors on the mat but a motley crew of jokesters off the mat—loud, boisterous, and constantly giving each other a hard time. In addition to Big Phil, a host of other comedians populated the team. Conversely, the Stanford wrestlers were polite and clean cut and a bit nerdy (I now consider "nerdy" the highest form of compliment and have converted into a full-blown, unapologetic nerd, by the way), but they were also confident and comfortable in their own skin.

I was first impressed by Scappy's ability to charm the waitress. Instead of ordering, he asked how she was, how her night was going. He listened intently as she confided that the dinner rush was crazy; she instantly loved him because he had the compassion and sensibility to treat her as a person rather than a servant. Scrappy explained that we were a group of hungry college wrestlers, and although the request seemed odd, would she mind bringing us each our own pitcher of water, as all of us were quite dehydrated? "Oh my Lord!" the waitress fawned. "Can we get these poor boys some water!" She was putty in his hands. As the meal progressed, I started to learn names and nicknames and did my best to play the role of my brother. It wasn't hard—I had spent every moment with him for eighteen years. Nevertheless, the lack of context kept tripping me up—names of people, places, etc.—but I managed to hold my own without doing too much damage.

I started to learn that this group of student athletes that I initially perceived as nerdy also possessed an amazing sense of humor. The Stanford wrestlers had a keen, delightful wit compared to the clowning, lowest-common-denominator digs of the Michigan crew. As the meal ended, we ordered coffee, and I caught onto something in this group that blew my mind. Instead of their treating the study session like a penance, I could tell that each of them was genuinely interested in the subject matter that he was reading. They talked about their goals and their futures, and you could not help but see that these kids were going places in life and that they were excited about the journey. The Stanford wrestlers were tough as nails in a different way. Each of them was hell-bent on proving that he could hang with the very best students at Stanford, despite having half the time and energy that a non-student-athlete would. At the same time, though they were not expected to come home with first place medals at a tournament as prestigious as the Midlands, they wanted to try their luck against the best, and by no means was this group going to take a backseat to the Michigan or Oklahoma State wrestlers with their multiplicity of coaches, superior funding, workout partners, and fancy uniforms. They would give their very best and go home proud of the effort. Given my voracious goals in high school and the intense, win-first atmosphere of wrestling at a Big Ten school, I had never viewed the sport this way. These guys put themselves through the trials and travails of Division I wrestling because they loved the sport—no other reason. Wrestling was a *part of their lives*, not their whole lives, and they had ample pursuits and interests outside the sport, which provided balance. I swear that that night a light bulb went on in my head. Although I was in the middle of the most childish, dishonest endeavor of my life, I left that restaurant with a different perspective as to whom Phil Nowick could actually be. Phil Nowick: college student, chaser of girls, ferocious Big Ten wrestler, or something else—something bigger and better.

As we retired to the hotel, my sole focus was to extract David and myself from this parallel universe. I cringed at how he had fared in my place and realized for the first time he must have had to take a reaming from my coaches for my failure. I knew the Michigan team was staying at the Marriott somewhere near the venue. I found a payphone in the hotel lobby, and after a few tries, I was able to locate the right Marriott. I was able to speak to David briefly. I could hear the relief in his voice; he was sweating bullets at this point and was convinced that he would actually have to *wrestle* in my place the next day. Or for that matter, maybe both of us feared deep down that we were doomed forever and would be forced to live out our lives as each other. I can tell you that was not going to happen. My brother was a premed major and, after I got a few looks at his organic chemistry text, forget it—I wasn't going near that stuff. Bizarro World David (me) would have to change his career pursuits.

It was 10:30 p.m., and Scrappy was getting ready to turn in. I told him I was going to the lobby to read a bit because I drank too much coffee at Denny's. I managed to take a cab over to the Marriott and found the right room. David (me) was rooming with Big Phil, and as I knocked on the room door, I could hear Big Phil bellow and laugh at something. My brother opened the door, and he was predictably shaken and furious when he saw it was me. I asked him to get a room key, and we walked to the hotel lobby. I apologized profusely and thanked him from the bottom of my heart—the MoonPie matter was settled, now and forever. We were square. We finally switched clothes again in the restroom of the lobby, and he made a hasty exit. I returned to my room (and my life), and I was relieved. As I nodded off to sleep, however, I could feel the bad karma kicking in. What I had done was a sacrilege to the sport of wrestling, and I imagined that the wrestling gods up there were angered. I was not wrong.

The first bit of vengeance kicked in as soon as I got out of bed at six in the morning. My calves were absolutely burning with soreness. The repetitive nature of simply sprinting up and down bleachers and steps for sixty minutes straight had caused a very large pulled muscle in one calf and a sore Achilles tendon in the other leg. I could barely walk. As we arrived at the arena and looked at the brackets to see who our first-round opponents would be, I got the last bit of comeuppance.

As with any type of sporting tournament, wrestlers always want their first-round opponent to be kind of a "warm-up" match. No one wants to face an NCAA champion in the first round—better to ease into the process and advance as far as you can before you bring out the heavy artillery. I gazed up at my opponent and was so shocked that I had to look twice. Guess what? I would be facing the number-one-seeded, top-ranked wrestler in the nation at my weight class (who would go on to win the NCAA title that year). To give some context as to his ability, he had easily handled Will Waters multiple times the year prior. I was not confused. For the first time in my life, I realized the very high probability that I was the warm-up opponent. To make matters worse, we were paired up in a "pigtail" round, meaning the loser would not wrestle again that day.

We arrived at the arena, and I began to go through my warm-up routine. I found my brother, and we drilled moves with each other. His first-round opponent was much more manageable, so my focus was trying to get him ready as I knew my fate was somewhat sealed. Drilling wrestling moves with my brother—even to this day at age forty—has always been my greatest joy in life. It was our way of understanding each other and helping each other through life. As we got into the rhythm of the drill session, I could tell he had forgiven me and that all was right with the universe. The buzzer sounded, and they asked the wrestlers to clear the mats. I patted David on the back and wished him good luck. They played the national anthem (which I always thought to be uncomfortable at 8:00 a.m. for some reason), and the very first matched announced was mine. There were only 3 or 4 pigtail-round matches—in which the wrestlers are essentially competing to get into the regular bracket—and only one mat was in use for this round, so literally the entire arena had no other options than to watch my match. As I arrived matside, I uttered the mantra of every severe underdog: "just do your best and give him hell." We shook hands, the referee blew the whistle, and I squatted then hit my best takedown as hard as I could. My legs were so sore and body so stiff that the entire attack was slow and awkward. My opponent countered immediately and spun around me with ease. Instead of riding me and trying for a pin, he immediately let me up and followed with a perfectly executed five-point takedown right to my back. Literally fifteen seconds had expired and I was down 7–1. After receiving back-points he let me up again and proceeded to take me down twice more in the period. My coaches cringed in my corner—I was not just losing, I was losing ugly, and they were none too pleased at having the entire arena watch one of their wrestlers get beat that way. I managed to survive the rest of the match without being pinned or losing by technical fall, but I put that match down as probably the most embarrassing performance of my wrestling career. My day was over before all of the other wrestlers had even started—the wrestling gods had spoken.

David ended up having a decent tournament, going 1–2, but he competed well and was satisfied that he had wrestled tough against some very high-level competition. On the bus ride home, my coaches informed me that in no way would I be given a challenge match for the varsity spot, and that if I could do no better than that performance at the Midlands, I should seriously rethink whether I was good enough to compete in the Big Ten at all.

That I did. As time went by and I finally made it over the hump, I developed into a wrestler that could compete at that level—at the Midlands, that is—but not in the Big Ten. I transferred to Stanford with my brother, and we resumed our life of drilling countless, blissful wrestling moves and experiencing the journey together. As I look back, that is all that mattered. The joy that I experienced in college wrestling stemmed from the experiences and friends that I made, not from championship medals. The winter break of my senior year I returned to the Midlands tournament. I placed fifth, with every other competitor in front of me having been an all-American or NCAA champion. This would be the *best* performance of my college career, and I was able to put the previous experience to rest.

I look back at the experience as somewhat transformative. My brief meal with my future teammates at Stanford somehow opened a window that allowed me to break out of the mold I had created for myself—one that clearly didn't fit. My own stupidity had unraveled into an experience that shook me off whatever track I was headed down. To this day I am amazed at the almost immediate negative impact of cutting corners or leaving things half-done. It's just not worth it. No matter what, if you do the right thing, it will always work in your favor.

Namaste.

STORY 7

(WAKE-UP) CALL 911

I know nothing, except the fact of my ignorance.
— Socrates

As I said, I have an innate knack for meandering into outlandish situations. Among the bizarre scenarios that I've managed to hook on the reel that I continually cast into the waters of life, this one is the whale. I was one of the lucky few in the physical building of the World Trade Center complex that made it out alive. What's more, after that first stroke of luck, I nevertheless found myself eighteen minutes later back at the scene within spitting distance of the South Tower as it collapsed. One singular image remains ingrained in my memory as I recount the experience: me, in gym clothes, running through the blinding smoke and debris, thinking *"I never got to coach wrestling with my twin brother."* My perceived last thought boiled down to that.

Three exceptional people (I think of them as *mensches*, but more on that in a minute) helped me unconditionally through the experience. The experience should have served as a cathartic wakeup call for me;

unfortunately it didn't, although in the long term I eventually found my way.

The saga begins at 2:30 a.m. on September 11, 2001, in the World Financial Center, global headquarters of Merrill Lynch, located at the lower tip of the West Side in Manhattan. I was working my life away into the wee hours of the night, a practice that had become standard operating procedure. The sport of wrestling had drifted far from my life and had been replaced by a much gloomier pursuit: I was a junior investment banker.

I am often fascinated by method actors (De Niro, Del Toro, Seymour Hoffman) who have difficulties snapping out of their acting roles once the production ends. The character, at some point, seeps into their actual being and takes the steering wheel in their life. For me, this insidious role was life on Wall Street, and now my every waking thought centered on moving up the brutally Darwinian pecking order at Merrill Lynch. I wasn't confused. At that point in the movie, I sat at rock bottom of the hierarchy, a single-celled amoeba.

Numerous offbeat qualities would encumber my evolution as a full-fledged investment banker. To begin with, I didn't hail from the right graduate school—a mammoth hindrance. Wall Street has a perverse attachment to pedigrees. Roughly 80 percent of my compatriots hailed from the Ivy League. I had garnered a law degree and masters in business at the University of Georgia. Although my alma mater boasts a solid business and law program, it is perhaps better known for superior barbecue, stunning coeds, and the perennial SEC powerhouse Georgia Bulldog football team. Not exactly a pipeline to Wall Street at the time. (I can still hear the open, disdainful laughter and sneers from my Yale, Harvard, and Columbia coworkers as I was introduced at associate training as "Phil Nowick, University of Georgia").

I certainly didn't look the part either. In stark contrast to the tall, distinguished stereotype, I looked like, well, a wrestler. I stood just above five feet tall (5'2" in the right shoes). My neck had long disappeared into my torso from years of weightlifting and grappling. I once greeted a key client at the bottom of the elevators at 250 Vesey. He showed me his identification and asked for a temporary pass. He thought I was security.

My disposition was a poor fit as well. I was continually told that I was far too nice to be an investment banker, that I somehow lacked the killer instinct. (Exactly who, I asked, was I supposed to kill? My coworkers, I guessed. Now that's team spirit). On one occasion, I was openly and publicly flogged for the unforgiveable offense of letting a twenty-one-year-old analyst escape the building. I found said analyst crying at his desk one night, totally broken in a sort of weepy, sleep deprived trance. He wailed incongruously in tongues. I was able to glean that he had strung together three consecutive "all-nighters" and was looking down the barrel of a fourth. I thought it a prudent decision to let this babbling mess of a young man go home and get some shut-eye. He would be more productive the next day. My senior managing director vehemently disagreed and expressed his displeasure in our Monday morning meeting, challenging my manhood in the public forum. (I think the term "Little F'ing Homo" was offered up as constructive criticism. Not good for my year-end evaluation). In any case, despite the obvious mismatch in character traits and appearance, at some point I got it stuck in my head that I would become an investment banker, even if it killed me. It almost did.

I had two redeeming qualities that served as an investment banking rip cord. I was darn good at the analytics (cash flow and valuation models on excel spreadsheets), and because I had a law degree, I could draft, read, understand, and negotiate contracts. Conversely, I was monumentally bad at making copies, graphic arts, and pushing pitch books through the bureaucracy of our word processing departments—70 percent of a junior banker's actual job. I abhorred ass-kissing. Nevertheless, despite being the equivalent of the kid with the booger-covered face on the investment banking playground, I always got picked for kickball—I could kick. Despite my irrelevance to office politics, I was able to attract a fairly good book of work by excelling at the core skills that clients actually demanded.

The above positive traits led to my most unbearably annoying habit for senior bankers—pointing out the truth. Managing directors in investment banking love to hear themselves speak. They live for fees, plastic deal toys, closing dinners, and the "scoreboard." If a client could be convinced to do a deal, that was immediately viewed in our circles as a savvy decision. No amount of self-congratulation was enough postclosing of the deal. Thus, having a devil's advocate in the room was blasphemy.

Upon completing a set of analytics, I would often point out that a contemplated transaction didn't work. Company X should not buy company Y; the price was too high. Piling debt upon company Z was the last thing they needed; the cash flow was sufficient to support a solid, small, unlevered business only. "Okay," my superiors would say, waving their hands at these insignificant facts, "simply change the model." Increase the profitability of the product, increase the rate and growth of sales, ratchet down the cost structure by increasing "synergies," and assume that company X could eventually sell company Y at a P/E ratio of fifteen, instead of thirteen. Voilá, you had fixed the actual company. At the transaction event, I would be assigned the role of inventing qualitative support, if asked.

As a passive aggressive act of defiance, I would do the work and then write a short memo. The blurb to my bosses would summarize our adjusted views but would also gently question the veracity of our new assumptions. I would subtly include a scenario analysis that bankers deftly label "the Downside Case" (which was, in truth, our realistic expectations for what the client could achieve). The reception was always violent: Are you saying you know more than us? Are you saying you know more about deals than [insert incarcerated CEO here]? "Idiot," one Director would say to me (that was his pet name for me), "we are trying to get paid. Do you want to get paid or give this deal to Lehman? They will tell the client whatever he wants to hear." I was no angel. I did want to get paid. I did want to cling to my job, and the actual transactions were interesting to me, so I would knuckle under and play the role of generic, voiceless, corporate enabler.

I begin the story at 2:30 a.m. because the prior day's work marathon resulted in approximately four hours of sleep and twenty slaps of the snooze button. As opposed to my usual 6:50 a.m., I awoke an hour late at 7:50 a.m. I had a choice to make: skip my morning workout (exercise aided me in functioning as a quasi-normal human on such limited sleep) or be on time for work. Because there is virtually no real quitting time on Wall Street—you get no brownie points for working late at night, a practice that is absolutely expected—the workday for investment bankers generally begins around 8:45 a.m.—a slight consolation. The people you see on CNBC at 6:00 a.m. are the traders, who generally end the day at market close, around 5:00 p.m. Bankers work much later hours, but correspondingly they begin a little later. Show up at 8:30 a.m., and the place is a ghost town. Show up at 9:00 a.m., and you are dead meat. I chose to tempt fate. I had worked until 3:00 a.m. I needed to work out for Pete's sake. I chronologically plotted my master plan. Ten minutes to pack up, that's 8:00 a.m.; fifteen minutes to make it to the Marriott World Trade Center health club, that puts me at 8:15 a.m.; a thirty minute run on the treadmill, I'm at 8:45 a.m.; five minute shower, 8:50 a.m. Immediately following, I would have to rush across the bridge back to World Financial, get lucky on the unbearably slow and hot elevator going up twenty-six floors, and, like a phantom, creep to my desk at around 9:05 a.m. All this was daunting but not impossible.

Per my usual morning practice, I rose from bed, pounded a thick brew of instant Chock Full o'Nuts coffee, and put on my gym gear. I then began to assemble my required Wall Street uniform. My dachshund, who we called Mousee (pronounced Mouse-eee) for her predilection to hide under furniture until she is rewarded with a treat, remained a lump under the covers and would not stir an inch. A designated representative from Personalized Pet Care by Alice would quietly let him or herself into my apartment and roust Mousee around 10:00 a.m., a time more to her liking, for the commute to the posh doggie day care located on the Lower East Side.

I packed two dress shirts from Barneys. Yes. You heard right—two shirts. Let me explain. Because I come from swarthy, sweaty, Eastern European Jewish stock, I would often, in the New York Fall humidity, sweat through the first shirt, postworkout, by 10:00 a.m. I can't stand wearing undershirts; I find them to be suffocating. Thus, as my first shirt generally dampened to the point of no return between 9:00 and 9:45 a.m., my nipples would start to shine through—much like Jennifer Anniston's nipples were prone to on the early episodes of *Friends* (highly acceptable for Jennifer, utterly not acceptable on Wall Street, to say the least).

In addition to my dual shirts, I gathered my Burberry suit, black dress socks, belt, power tie, and dress shoes into a suit bag, which I would hold in my right hand. My gym bag with shower supplies and a towel would be slung over my right shoulder. In my left hand, I would drag a rolling briefcase with my array of electronics—including my laptop and beloved Blackberry (a device I have grown to despise)—and work papers (contracts, credit agreements, draft pitch books, excel spreadsheets, offering circulars, etc.). To boot, the rolling briefcase contained every piece of identification that I owned. "Why consolidate a birth certificate, passport, driver's license, and selective service card all into one place?" you ask. I'll give you a classic answer—it seemed like a good idea at the time. I had been traveling quite a bit to Mexico City, and I was paranoid that I would lose my identification and become some sort of gringo fugitive, so I overcompensated a bit.

My daily morning expedition consisted of a trek down South End Avenue in Battery Park City, into the Winter Garden, across the enclosed bridge to the World Trade Center, and up the elevator eleven floors to the

Marriott World Trade Center health club. The journey was the walking equivalent of five city blocks and took fifteen minutes. To the average resident of Los Angeles, Denver, or Miami, a journey of this magnitude for a thirty-minute morning workout, toting three bags in various states of wrap around my body, might seems excessive. I assure you, though, for New Yorkers, the practice is not the slightest bit out of the norm. One of the downsides to traveling exclusively by foot, cab, and subway is that New Yorkers have zero receptacles for their stuff. So, over time, residents of the Big Apple adjust to packing up like Juan Valdez's trusty burro most places they go from nine to five. I was no exception.

My morning run was surprisingly good at the health club. Just as I had planned, I stepped on the treadmill at 8:15 a.m. The facility sat at the top of the Marriot World Trade Center hotel and boasted a large floor area with a breathtaking view of the Hudson. My morning workouts were generally the closest thing to pleasant in an otherwise grueling workday. I even hired the resident boxer trainer from time to time, and he often would cap off our workouts with stair runs via what functioned as the emergency exit. I broke a nice sweat on September 11. I was experiencing one of those runs that unfolded nicely. I felt alert, loose, and limber despite my lack of sleep.

Pleasant thoughts rolled through my head, mostly because I patently refused to think of work during my exercise. The Denver Broncos, my hometown team, had won easily versus the Giants the night before in the season opener on Monday Night Football. I had missed the game—I had to work—but checked the score constantly online the night before. Ed McCaffrey, our gritty, fan-favorite receiver, had broken his leg in gruesome fashion. Tough loss, I thought. My twin brother's wedding was coming up; he would complete his residency soon in anesthesia. I needed to get on the ball for that bachelor party. The Back Street Boys played in the background on the health club speaker—please end, song; just end. I wondered if I could get Jennifer, the brown-eyed Broadway actress, to call me back if I got hold of tickets for *The Producers*—everybody said it was good. The time of 8:45 a.m. rolled around before I knew it, and I reluctantly stepped off the treadmill. I generally allotted 5–6 minutes to mosey around the club for my favorite part of the day, the cooldown—just sit there and sweat, clear my head. Mentally prepare for …

At 8:46 a.m., the sound of the explosion came straight from hell. It was deafening and alien, as if God had clashed together two cymbals the size of mountains. The dreadful reverberations spewed auditory hate and lasted for what seemed like an eternity. That's what I remember most—the sound of the crash. The building shook violently, and I hit the deck like a commando in an army movie. I looked up. The young woman at the front desk somehow maintained her composure and pointed to the emergency stairs. I was less than five feet away—talk about fortunate. Having completed a good number of wind sprints up those stairs, I didn't hesitate, and I bolted through the exit. The stairs were already crowded with hotel patrons. Nobody panicked. This was New York, these things happened. The unshaken demeanor of the random group immediately reassured me, and we all jogged in an orderly fashion down the scant eleven flights of stairs. "Got to be a bomb," I heard one man say. "Damn Arabs bombed the Trade Center again." I hit the ground floor and burst into the hazy autumn sunlight. Fire trucks and police had already arrived on the scene. In what would be a continuing theme, I opted, with many other shocked New Yorkers, to stand and stare upward instead of fleeing.

The disaster, although hideous, looked contained at first. I sat on the opposite side of the collision point on the South Tower and could not necessarily see the extent of the damage. I asked a firefighter, who also comically underestimated the events to come, what had happened. "Some kook flew a plane into the building," he said. "Big plane or little plane?" I asked. "You know, like a Cessna?" "Little one, I think," the mistaken firefighter replied. Instead of shock and compassion for the victims several floors up, my thoughts drifted selfishly toward work. I was exceedingly late for work, and my wallet, cell phone, and precious

Blackberry were stuck upstairs in the health club locker room. Surely they would put this fire out eventually. I asked the firefighter when I would I be able to go back up the Marriott stairs and retrieve my stuff. "Stick around," the firefighter said, "we'll let you know." I did—which commenced a series of dim-witted decisions that, like a moth to a flame, kept bringing me back to the epicenter of the attack. (For future reference, I would advise readers that, if a terrorist attack of any kind occurs in your vicinity, you should run away immediately and keep running).

"How am I going to explain this?" I thought. The latest version of a cash flow model (one that had resulted from countless sleepless nights) for our Mexican client, a copper tubing manufacturer, resided on my laptop, which was currently being held hostage. I was so screwed. I muddled through the conundrum in my head and imagined my caustic superiors asking why, pray tell, the model was not on their desks. First full-fledged terrorist attack ever on US soil: solid excuse. Beginning my workout at 8:15 a.m., hoping to sneak into work: not so sound. I finally made a command decision. I would need to walk back to my apartment in Battery Park City, shower, dress, and walk into work hopelessly tardy and empty-handed. How the hell am I going to pay for lunch? I asked myself as I crossed the West Side Highway toward the harbor. I swam upstream back to my apartment, crossing paths with countless professionals heading into work despite the gore in plain sight.

I finally reached my apartment at precisely 9:03 a.m. How do I know the exact timing with such specificity? Because the moment I opened my mouth asking our friendly doorman for a spare key to apartment 7H at 377 Rector Place, the second unforgettable sound came. It was a malevolent screech, the kind you hear at airports if you sit too close to the runway. Even before the second deafening boom of the North Tower collision occurred, I did the math in my head. *The noise was a plane, a big one. That first plane was not, in fact, a Piper Cub or Cessna; it was much larger. The horrid sound above you now is a 747—its twin. This is a large-scale terrorist attack radiating from the Middle East, possibly from that one guy that Clinton tried to bomb. More planes are likely coming. You are in grave danger. The time to panic would be now.*

And then the second explosion came. It seemed twice as loud and twice as long as the first. I again dropped to my knees. As the sound subsided, I staggered to my feet and ran outside my apartment building. I now viewed—instead of jaded New Yorkers toughing it out to work—bedlam: people grabbing their hair and crying, people running in circles, pushing and colliding into each other. Everybody else on the street, the rest of New York, and the entire nation had also done the math that quickly, and they were similarly panicked. I found one of my neighbors, Mr. Roth, a sixtyish man from the fourth floor with whom I often intersected on dog walks, lying flat on the sidewalk.

I helped Mr. Roth to his feet. I feared he had suffered a heart attack, but he had simply been knocked to the ground as people initially scattered from the explosion. I grabbed his arm, and we walked for awhile down the normally serene stretch of walk overlooking the harbor. We really didn't say much for a few minutes. He began trying to reach his wife and daughter by cell phone. At that point, both Twin Towers remained standing, including their cellular beacons—not for long. After Mr. Roth had recovered from his fall a bit, we walked further east. The Statue of Liberty stood in full view—even she looked a little freaked out. Army vehicles started to populate South End Avenue, and we began to hear murmurs in the crowd that everybody would be evacuated on military barges across the harbor to New Jersey. "Forget that," Mr. Roth said. I agreed, and we made an inexplicable pact to recross the West Side Highway toward the towers. We traversed countless emergency vehicles as we made our way to the other side. Our goal was, like the rest of America, to find our way to a TV and discern what was going on. Looking back, we could have picked a better location.

At approximately 9:55 a.m., we stopped at the southwest corner of the World Trade Center complex on Church Street, just north of Liberty.

Geographically speaking, we were staring straight up at the South Tower. Someone had placed a radio in the middle of the street, and a very large crowd gathered around. The announcer breathlessly recounted the two attacks on the Towers (American Airlines Flight 11 and United Airlines Flight 175), the crash at the Pentagon (American Airlines Flight 77), and the final travesty in a field in Pennsylvania (United Airlines Flight 93). Flames and thick, putrid smoke now gushed from both Towers; large chunks of building fell to the ground.

As I said before, I remember the sounds of the experience as much as the visions. A horrifying collective scream directed my attention upward. We then watched as, one by one, several people took their own lives leaping from the blaze. The next sound I distinctly remember was the sickened weeping of a woman standing next to me—to quote the Hindenburg experience, "Oh, the humanity!" Even though I had a front row seat, my experience was no different from yours watching on TV. I stood completely still and simply stared, in a state of hypnosis, at the carnage unfolding.

Finally, Mr. Roth broke our silence and said, "I'm getting out of here. I'm meeting my wife at my sister's house on the Upper East Side. Come with…" He stopped midsentence, turned his back to me, and started running away. Everybody started running away.

I never saw him again. I also never saw the South Tower crumble. I just followed suit with the herd and started hoofing it myself. I erroneously assumed that a third plane was approaching. I was dressed perfectly for the occasion: black New Balance running shorts, ASICS running shoes, thin running socks, and a navy-blue Nike performance top—time to perform, I guessed. I exploded north on Church Street, passing people in heels and pedestrian work shoes by the dozen. I then hit a hard right on Fulton Street. My plan was still based on the premise that a third plane was coming: get away from the tall buildings, best to head east a bit. I hit Broadway and turned north, running top speed. At this point I heard the earsplitting cacophony of the South Tower collapsing. Within fifteen seconds, a blanket of blinding, smoldering, wretched smoke from the fallen equivalent of a small city then enveloped lower Manhattan. I literally breathed in pure debris. Forward visibility was absolute zero. As I ran, I felt an instant of deflation and loss because I rationally assumed I would die in this hateful fog.

Most people encountered with a similar experience would, I'm guessing, choose something like the following for their last thought on earth: "I will never fall in love again." "I'll never see my beautiful wife and kids again." "I wish I would have told my dad I love him." I assume that's fairly typical. My last thought was a bit different. I was thirty-one years old and had dated chronically via online grab bags such as JDate and Match.com, which solidly knocked out the first two of the above options. But I had, in fact, matured to the point that I had told my father, Martin, that I loved him, so the third didn't apply to me either. No, my apparent last thought was the following: *"I never got to coach wrestling with my twin brother."* In retrospect, it didn't exactly take Socrates to discern what life was telling me.

I kept running. My lungs burned like wildfire from the air quality, the adrenaline, and the physical exertion. I was scared out of my mind. But, in a strange way, I was prepared for this moment. I had dealt with fear, and I had persevered through extreme fatigue countless times on the wrestling mat. I mentally transported back in time to the red practice room at my high school. "Suck it up," I heard my high school Coach Steve Foster bellow. "Pain is fear leaving the body. Keep going." I did, and I made it out of that goddamn smoke alive.

Completely exhausted, I finally slowed my pace, stopping at 317 Broadway in front of a McDonalds. I glimpsed myself in the storefront window. I looked like some sort of Shakespearian ghost. I was completely covered head-to-toe in chunky, white soot. I also really had to pee. I walked inside the McDonalds and found a long line in front of the restroom. Like-colored ghouls in the form of businessmen, hotdogs vendors, secretaries, and other walks of life, we all waited somberly to wash the death from our faces. No one said a word. We just looked in one another's countenances with a mix of compassion and dread. By the time I reached the bathroom, the sink had accumulated a thick layer of sludge. I still couldn't believe what I saw in the mirror.

Having done my best to wash up and with bladder relieved, I stepped out of the McDonalds and stood in a daze in the September heat for a solid five minutes. I found it surreal that time and life, after such a horrible tragedy, stubbornly refused to skip a beat. I looked inside the restaurant, and they were still flipping burgers. A bus drove by. Apparently the driver, not knowing what else to do, felt a sense of duty to keep to his route. I ambled around the lower portion of Manhattan in a trance. What was I supposed to do next? The answer came to me in a single, simple posttraumatic thought: "I wonder if Mousee"—my pet dachshund and canine soul mate—"is dead." Personalized Pet Care by Alice, the classy pet day care service run by the self-professed "Doggie Diva," Alice Moss, generally picked up Mousee midmorning. I tried not to let that thought enter my mind. Sometimes they came early. I had to find out. My single purpose became to discover the fate of my brown-eyed angel. I remembered the location of Alice's: Essex, between Broome and Delancey. I started walking and at some point got lost in The Bowery and had to ask directions, but I eventually found it.

Personalized Pet Care by Alice was an enchanting three-story tenement located at 83 Essex. Alice Moss and her husband—the two of whom seemed very much in love—lived on the top floor. The second floor of their converted apartment was reserved for big dogs (I always marveled at the popularity of horse-sized dogs in Manhattan, where space was so limited). The first floor housed the small to midsize dogs. Like all of her two-legged clients, I developed a strong affinity for Alice, although I had only met her briefly. She loved all of her customers, human and canine, with the intensity of an overbearing but wonderful aunt. She had boarded Mousee many times during my business trips, and she called frequently—unsolicited—to let me know about my dog's well-being. Alice's equally personable employees traversed Manhattan in a comically large van (a converted ice cream truck, I think) early every morning and late every evening, picking up and dropping off people's trusted canine companions. I marveled at Alice's life. She lived in a state of utter disarray, dogs everywhere. Yet she derived a robust sense of joy from spoiling her four-legged clients rotten from dawn until dusk.

Time for the truth. As I pressed the buzzer on the ground floor, I realized that life boiled down to two realities for me: Mousee was either sitting on the first floor at that moment, and things would be okay, or she was stuck in my apartment and would perish, a reality that I still refused to contemplate. A crackly voice escaped from the speaker box, "Yes?" "It's Phil Nowick," I responded hastily. "I'm Mousee's owner." "Oh my God!" a new voice, Alice's, replied, "I'll be right down." That didn't sound good; I waited in agony. The heavy, metal security door screeched open. Out popped Alice and in her arms, like an infant, was a small, brown bundle of joy. "We picked her up early today, thank God!" I started to cry, my heart filled with relief and delight. Everything would be okay.

The word that comes to mind when I think of Alice is "*mensch*." For those of you unfamiliar with Yiddish jargon, a *mensch* is an exceptionally kind, affable, and generous person. Alice's face would appear on the front cover of the *mensch* handbook, if such a resource existed. Alice invited me inside and asked if I had anywhere to stay. I hadn't thought about it. "You can't go back there (meaning downtown). You'll stay with us. Let's get you cleaned up." I was in no place to argue; I simply clung to Mousee and followed this kindhearted woman inside. At around 10:30 a.m., after hundreds of attempts to establish a phone connection, I was able to reach my family and put their fears at ease. I was fine, I told them; I escaped the harrowing experience with merely a skinned knee, nothing else—I was lucky. No, I was not mentally traumatized, I lied, both to my family and to myself. I did not need to seek counseling or help.

I awoke on Wednesday, September 12, in a pile of small to midsize dogs. The bed that Alice very graciously provided to Mousee and me was apparently community property. A veritable melting pot of breeds shared our slumber. Pugs, poodles, beagles, schnauzers—name any kind of dog and it was probably snoozing on top of me. I was covered in hair, and Alice offered to wash my gym clothes … again. I accepted and changed into one of her husband's bathrobes. I was invited upstairs to the living quarters and noticed a computer resting on the kitchen table. A light bulb went on in my head. I should probably check my e-mail. My work e-mail was not accessible, as it resided on a secure corporate server that had just been blown to smithereens. I opted for my Yahoo! account and found in the vicinity of 300 e-mails in my in-box. All of the messages took the form of desperation and touching concern for my well-being. Schoolmates, coworkers, ex-girlfriends, and family all sent some form of note wishing to confirm my safety. I guessed I had my work cut out for me in responding.

One e-mail caught my eye; it went something like this (I couldn't track down the exact e-mail): "Phil. I hope you are okay. Are you able to go home? I heard Battery Park City is trashed. Let me know if you need a place to stay. Karen."

Karen was my friend Karen Robinovitz. If the name sounds familiar, yes, we are talking about *the* Karen Robinovitz: renowned writer, pop culture guru, book author, celebrity interviewer, TV fashion commentator, corporate branding consultant, movie screenwriter and producer … and double *mensch*. If Alice would have been on the cover of the aforementioned handbook, Karen would have written it. It would become a best seller. The front cover would be pink.

Karen did not yet have *the* attached to her name as a permanent prefix in 2001; she had not quite reached superstardom, but she was right on the cusp. She was managing only three careers at that point, as compared with her current ten or more at any one moment. At that time, her three vocational areas of focus, based on my observations, were a) writing b) bullet points and c) shoe shopping, the latter two of which were inextricably entwined. Let me explain.

Karen's first career, which comprised a majority of her working time (24/7), was writing. Karen would generally wake up early, throw on some sweats, grab a smoothie from a trendy West Village juice bar, and return to her home (which functions as a working office). Properly fueled, she would then sit down at her computer and commence composing brilliance: scrumptious fashion, investigative articles or celebrity pieces for the A-list of weekly or daily periodicals. Her roster of high-profile employers included: *The New York Times*, the *New York Post*, *Marie Claire*, *Harper's Bazaar*, *Elle*, *Mademoiselle*, *City*, *Details*—the list goes on forever. Karen's appeal as an author was her innate sense of the current pulse of pop culture—what was hot—and a fast-hitting, enjoyable writing style. Some of her articles could be branded avant-garde or, more accurately in my opinion, downright ballsy. One of her more famous pieces was titled "Secrets to a Sixty Minute Orgasm," the subject matter of which was a self-proclaimed sex guru in New York. Karen's editors had requested a "fly-on-the-wall" type of observation, but Karen retorted that there was no way to verify the veracity of this person's claim other than her style of observation: hands-on. The article was a smash hit. From a monetary standpoint, I think Karen did very well and used the wages from her first career for everyday items: savings, meals, bills, furniture, travel, etc.

Karen's second career—again by my observation—took no more than 5 percent of her working time but was highly lucrative. Many popular magazines for which she wrote, such as *Marie Claire*, often made requests of Karen, not for articles per se, but for *bullet points*. If Karen was the Mozart of fashion writing, she was the Bobby Fischer of bullet points: top five budding celebrities you would hear of in the coming year, top ten ways to propose to your fiancé in New York, top five no-no's on a first date, top ten new Ethiopian restaurants in the Manhattan area, top five ways to know if your dominatrix is right for you, and on that note, top five places to buy quality but affordable leather garments, top five ways to become a sex goddess in less than one week, etc. This process was absolutely fascinating. Every few hours, a frenzied magazine editor would call or e-mail in a panic and ask Karen to produce some sort of unconventional list magically: "I need the top ten things women hate in bed but will never tell you, by 3:00 p.m.!" Fair enough, Karen would calmly respond, and in the ensuing sixty seconds, she would hit send on her e-mail—bullet points done. She was like Dustin Hoffman's character in *Rain Man*, but with bullet points instead of baseball statistics. Bullet points simply flowed like manna from heaven out of Karen's consciousness. A check would arrive from the requesting magazine at Karen's West Village address 2–5 days later. One hundred percent of the proceeds, it seemed, were dedicated to Karen's third career: shoes.

Karen was the Warren Buffett of shoes. I do not want to paint the picture of some amateur compulsive shopper, because that would do injustice to her art. Like the "Oracle of Omaha," she invested in large chunks, but with unbreakable patience. Before acting, Karen ensured that she was armed with complete information, based on intensive research, at all times. Karen's mind was able to assimilate, compare, and contrast, at any given moment, the entire shoe inventory in her size of every high-fashion boutique in Manhattan. Like a trader on the T-Bond desk at Merrill, she would receive several calls daily from inside sources on the status of the market. Owners and employees of such boutiques regarded her as a type of demagogue, not only because she was the "perfect ten" of customers but, in addition, because she was a budding celebrity, knew many celebrities, and had inside information on the competition.

Also like Buffett, Karen was not afraid to use her clout to pull off ruthless trades. She had a spider sense for shoe sales, and was accordingly able to execute a rare form of shoe arbitrage. Karen would wait until the last possible instant to remove a price tag and let a pair of shoes actually touch her feet—only after she had extracted the last ounce of value. As an example, let's hypothesize that Karen initially purchased a pair of Jimmy Choo black strappy heels at full retail price in November.

Furthermore, we'll assume that the same pair of shoes in alternative colors, in the exact same size and style, subsequently went on sale after the holiday rush. Karen would sense a disturbance in the shoe force and immediately return the black pair of Choos in exchange for three of the newly discounted pairs. Although I never saw it, I imagined her selling two of the pairs to a short list of like-size friends at a reasonable price. As a result, Karen, in my mind, would end up with her preferred pair of shoes in her favorite color without, at the end of the day, having expended a single dollar.

The most impressive part of Karen's exploits was that, in stark contrast to my pursuits, Karen's work, personal life, and inner circle brought out the best in her. She literally shined. Part of her magnetism is that she is the extremely rare individual whose spirit animal resides in her career. When she had so many people clawing at her time, how did I, a C-level investment banker, luck into a friend like Karen? We dated for a very brief period (an old-fashioned Jewish set-up); otherwise, no way she would have gone out with me under normal circumstances.

To this day, our first date was the best I have ever experienced for two reasons. First, Karen is actually an inch shorter than I, which made me instantly love her. Second, like all good first dates, the conversation migrated toward professional wrestling within the first ten minutes. Karen, as a young girl growing up in South Florida, jettisoned Barbie dolls in favor of watching Georgia Championship Wrestling—Sundays on the Turner Network. We exchanged views: I favored Ric Flair and the Road Warriors; she fancied "Wildfire" Tommy Rich and the The Fabulous Freebirds. She asked if I ever turned pro what my stage name would be. That was easy. "The Hebrew Crippler," I replied. She was thrilled and offered to quit her job as a writer and serve as my ringside valet if I ever made the switch. I never had the guts.

Back to her e-mail. Without hesitation, I accepted Karen's bighearted offer for me and my dachshund (Mousee adored Karen) to stay at her place until I could find alternative residence. Her message was correct.

The Army was now camped out in Battery Park City as if it were wartime Beirut, and the air quality made the neighborhood unfit for habitation. I would not make it back to my apartment for another four weeks. As I changed into my newly clean gym clothes, I started to understand the most crucial collateral damage of the prior day's event. I had lost my identity, completely. Every piece of paper that somehow marked my existence on the planet had burned in my briefcase. I had no wallet, no driver's license, no passport, no cell phone, no Blackberry, etc. Additionally, I had amassed financial resources in savings, checking, and investment accounts, but those things existed, not as hard currency, but as concepts in cyberspace. Phil Nowick, in a statistical sense, needed to identify himself in some form, or to possess a specific type of plastic, magnetic card to access such funds. Functionally speaking, I was a nobody without a penny to my name.

This should have been an awe-inspiring and liberating moment. I should have realized that certain events—a life-threatening illness, a nuclear attack, a meteor collision with the Earth, an alien space landing, or the Oakland Raiders winning the Super Bowl—could result in chaos and change the fabric of human existence in a heartbeat. At such a point in time, the roles we play and the toys that we have hoarded mean nothing. All that is left is … *us*. Our heartbeat, our breath, our love that we have for each other, the stories we have created—*that's it*. Instead of contemplating this momentous state, one single, shallow thought replicated itself like a computer virus over and over in my head: "I've got to get hold of my ATM card." Although I lacked the maturity and requisite soul to pick up on it all, someone, something—life, God, call it what you want—was trying pretty hard to get my attention and lay it all out for me. "We are taking it all away for a moment. Did you see how happy Alice Moss was? We are sending you to your friend Karen, who has also found her path. Please observe, make the appropriate changes, and get back to us." As I said, I missed the ball completely.

Karen gave me her address, and I set out a plan to make the journey from the Lower East Side to the West Village. Policemen guarded every single corner in Manhattan. The city was locked down, as the world tried to make sense of the situation. Identification was required at every juncture. As I ventured out—receiving a crushing, teary-eyed bear hug from Alice on my way out—lacking proof of my identity, I enacted an alternative strategy. I placed Mousee on my shoulder and started walking. To every objectionable officer that stopped me, I plainly stated that no terrorist would be caught dead while travelling with a one-year-old brown dachshund. It would ruin the tough guy image, I reasoned. Al-Qaeda would never hear of it. The strategy worked.

The next three days at Karen's were blissful. I had not taken a day off of work in quite some time, and I was able to decompress as we frequented her favorite spots—her boxing trainer, her juice bar, her five favorite sushi restaurants. Karen certainly knew how to enjoy life, and it was fun riding along. I still didn't have a change of clothes, and we continued with the routine of washing the same pair of gym gear while I sat in a pair of her pink pajamas. Beyond that, I spent every ounce of my time calling Merrill Lynch (also my financial institution for regulatory purposes), searching for a way for my beloved ATM card to find its way home. The card arrived at Karen's address on the third day of my stay. (I will give Merrill credit for one thing: they bent over backward to help accommodate displaced employees after 9/11). I tore open the envelope, signed the back, and Karen and I proceeded to the nearest machine. My heart started to sing at the familiar *thwack, thwack, thwack* of twenty-dollar bills dispensing. Any spiritual revival that I perhaps had begun to experience ended there.

I immediately started consuming. I remarked to Karen, "I guess I better get some clothes." I suggested Banana Republic or Gap for starters. Karen gave me a revolted look and laughed. "Come with me," she said. We took a cab to the hottest boutique in Manhattan—Jeffrey, in the Meatpacking District. Within five minutes, I had blown through my entire mental budget for a wardrobe on one pair of Prada boots. Between Paper Denim & Cloth jeans, Armani turtlenecks, Jil Sander knits and button-ups, and several pairs of curiously expensive socks and underwear, I purchased the equivalent of a new Kia automobile in garments. Karen beamed with pride. I had made the transformation from dumpily dressed banker to full-fledged, high-fashion New York hipster (a look now commonly referred to as modern douche bag). We dined at SUSHISAMBA that night—a chic fusion restaurant: Japanese and Cuban food. The ecstasy would end there, however. Merrill Lynch had left a message for me on Karen's machine. The substance of the message was this: enough whining and grieving, we all needed to get our butts back to work.

The World Financial Center—my former workplace—had been temporarily condemned. In response, Merrill Lynch had orchestrated the brilliant maneuver of securing the similarly empty 222 Broadway for our working pleasure. The former tenants of the building had fled like cockroaches exposed to light because the location sat directly adjacent to Ground Zero. Merrill Lynch glossed over our relocation as a show of patriotism—that, unlike our wimpy brethren at Lehman Brothers and Deutsche Bank, we would not be chased from lower Manhattan. Thick smoke still billowed out of the former tower sites for weeks, generating a stench of dust, concrete, and, quite literally, human remains both inside and out of our new location. For our viewing pleasure, in the cafeteria on the top floor, the several thousand employees scarred by scampering from the terrorist attack a few days before were treated to a panoramic scene of bulldozers unearthing a mass grave.

My first day back to work at Merrill Lynch was one of my last. The day kicked off to a cheery start in the leveraged finance group—my group—with a rousing speech from our fearless leader (we'll call him Chad, for now). Chad stood up on a chair for some reason, dispensed with any chitchat, and boldly announced that in less than thirty days more than half of us would be laid off. Those of us that wished to stay better work damn hard to drum up some business. (Let's forget the fact that the whole financial world had just been stomped out as if it were a bug. No one was interested in a new facility, floating some high yield bonds, or purchasing their competitors in a leveraged buyout). Chad was a "bottom-line guy," he boasted. We would generate fees—right now—or be terminated. Wow! Talk about inspiring … JFK had nothing on this guy.

Chad sported a $3,000 shiny-gray Armani suit and a dark-tan European shirt with a chunky, black tie that day … his standard costume. His face was absurdly gaunt because he had far overdone the whole Atkins thing—just looking at him made you want to shove a funnel cake down his throat. Chad's overall visual impression was that of some sort of malnourished mafioso. His demeanor embodied the very worst of investment bankers: effete, arrogant beyond belief, with a highly distorted sense of ethics. Upon completing his pep talk, Chad strode up to me in full view of everyone and, in a sociopathic effort to feign the appearance of the compassionate leader, said the following: "Phil, (he had never spoken a word to me in over a year of working in his group of thirty bankers, and he had required the assistance of a younger banker to identify just who this Phil Nowick idiot was) we were all worried about you," he said. "It took us a long time to track you down. But I want to convey one thing to you, loud and clear. If you had been at your desk at eight forty five this never would have happened." True story. I balled up my fists at my side and almost swung. Instead, I swallowed the insult whole, like the thousands of others I had endured on Wall Street the four years prior. I left the room and ducked into a stairwell. I actually tried to cry, but nothing came out—such would be the case for the next seven years of my life.

I returned to the room and stumbled to my newly assigned cubicle. I picked up the phone and began listening to over fifty of my voice messages that Merrill Lynch had recovered in the phone system from September 11. Like the e-mails I had opened days before, most of the voicemails were from friends and relatives, all thickly laced with panic. Had I made it out of the building? Was I okay? God bless, please call.

The very first message on my voicemail was from a dear friend named Larry Mizel. If that name, too, sounds vaguely familiar, Larry is a Denver-based, billionaire real estate magnate and world-renowned philanthropist. Larry is a type of *übermensch*, both taking his time to counsel young people individually and using his largesse to help with the world's most challenging causes. He had served as a mentor to me since I was eighteen, after a very random introduction from my Grandpa Sid. Larry took a liking to me, despite my erratic, youthful tendencies, because he, too, was a wrestler. Larry grew up in Tulsa, Oklahoma, where, to this day, by city ordinance, you wrestle growing up. "We are worried about you, Phil. Please call." Six days after his message, I did.

Larry had already received confirmation from my parents that I was intact. Out of nowhere, without a single moment of thought, I asked him for a job. Could I come home to Denver? Paradoxically, it was Larry who had strongly urged me to attend law school, to obtain a joint degree with an MBA, and to start my career on Wall Street. He would now be my salvation from that life. "Sure. We'll find something for you to do, but I want you to take a month off first. We'll see you after that." No contract, no offer/counteroffer, just simply, "Of course, see you in a month." Welcome home.

"By the way, you still wrestling?" he asked.

"Not lately," I replied, "but I plan to change that soon."

"Good," he said, and he hung up the phone.

There is no uplifting ending to this story in the short term—quite the opposite. In the ensuing months, which bled into years, I slipped like a bad method actor even deeper into my false role, even further away from wrestling. In an effort to repay Larry for his years of kindness, I pursued my career with a—and this is the appropriate word—vengeance. I kept on consuming, in addition to pursuing other various false idols bereft of soul to cover the pain of my experience on 9/11. Although, in theory,

I had begun coaching wrestling again with my twin brother, my travel scheduled rendered me a no-show at 90 percent of our practices. The illumination that wrestling gave me burned dangerously low. Coming within inches of death on 9/11 apparently was not enough of a wake-up call. The images that appeared to me as I fled through the smoke did not hit home. It would take a much larger, much more violent alarm a few years later to stir me finally from my slumber into consciousness. Don't worry, I finally end up getting it, but it would take a few years.

I have indirectly hammered at the resounding moral to this story and book, so I won't belabor the point. To surmise, the moment I took some time in my life and started redefining success, I was truly able to change: joy flooded in, and I became a *mensch* in training. To date, I aspire to be a *successful* wrestling coach, friend, father to my three insatiable dachshunds, brother, son, mentor to young kids, etc. Yes, I have some other highly defined skills in other areas of life, but I don't fool myself—my exploitation of these talents is not true success. It merely sets the table in terms of providing practical needs that pave the way, so I don't sweat them too much. *Wrestling brings the light.*

Namaste.

EPILOGUE

Forks in the road form spider webs
in front of us each and every day.
— *Phil Nowick, author*

Phil did fulfill his destiny. Phil did achieve his dream of becoming a mensch. He found the productive pursuit that brought joy to him. It came from sharing the fun in his life. Coaching wrestling, with the help of his twin brother, Dave, was what he loved and what made people love him.

In October, 2008, Phil found himself caught up in the biggest spider web of his life. "What," you ask, "could have been a more devastating experience than barely escaping the 9/11 explosions and the difficult afterlife in New York City?" The answer is *cancer*. Phil was diagnosed with stage four colon cancer after he had become very ill and sought medical care. The path of this web started with immediate, extensive abdominal surgery to remove the tumors found in his colon. Six weeks following surgery, Phil began the first of twelve intensive chemotherapy sessions. Many consultations, body scans, and research for the best treatment ensued. The cancer therapy continued torturously and ploddingly into May of 2009.

Phil was adamant about making a complete recovery. The doctors gave him a good chance for beating the cancer. So, just like when he was conditioning to beat a fearsome opponent in a future wrestling tournament or preparing to execute a complicated financial transaction, Phil put all of his energy, concentration, and intellect into reclaiming a healthy body. Phil had a new diet, a new exercise routine, and a new passion for experiencing the good things in his life. He was helped by many family members, friends, and therapy professionals. Lots of people gave him encouragement and support. Most importantly, everyone prayed.

Phil was used to being strong and winning. He was a standout wrestler at Cherry Creek High School in Colorado. Even today, he ranks among the top three on the all-time win list with 114 varsity victories. He placed four times at the CHSAA State Wrestling Championship, twice reaching the finals. After high school, he went on to wrestle for the University of Michigan and then for Stanford University. At Stanford, where he earned his bachelor's degree in economics, he was a three-year NCAA Division I starter at 118 pounds. For his graduate studies, Phil attended the University of Georgia, earning a law degree and an MBA. He continued success with a career in finance for five years in New York with Morgan Stanley and Merrill Lynch and then seven years in Colorado with MDC Holdings and PNT Capital.

As the cancer treatment continued, Phil looked for activities to fill his sedentary life. Of course, this included wrestling. He could not actually complete wrestling maneuvers because of the weakness caused by the cancer treatments, but he could teach them. His days began to fill with research for ways to show how he could coach wrestling. Purler Wrestling Academy, founded by Nick and Tony Purler, provided just the kind of expertise and support that Phil was seeking. Phil closed his investment advisor office, PNT Capital, and put all his effort toward preparing to coach wrestling with youth groups.

In the summer of 2009, Phil became stronger. He was working out with kettlebells and increasing his endurance with Yoga and other exercising. In July, on the order of his doctor, Phil went through a complete body scan. The call came two days later. "Phil, there is no evidence of cancer," the doctor said. What elation Phil felt. He could live again as he had before, without fear. His path was headed out of the darkness. He was so thankful for the power of God intervening in his life and to all who had helped him. He was free to follow his passion: wrestling.

"The happiest times of my life," Phil maintained, were the months following his cancer-free body scan. Phil founded Purler Wrestling Rocky Mountain and formed three youth wrestling groups. He was busy and thrilled with the new challenge of coaching. He felt joy in giving of himself to others. The groups met twice a week for practice and coaching sessions, sometimes with his brother, Dave's, help. Phil also coached at a private high school. New friends and old relationships flooded into his life. His wrestling program netted five Tulsa National placers and two Tulsa National champions in the first year of existence.

Then it happened. Just as he had written about in the stories, Phil's life path took a hard left turn. In January, 2010, Phil felt really sick and exhausted. He was unable to do his usual activities. Finally admitting he needed medical assistance, he visited his doctor. Tests revealed the impossible. Cancer had returned. How could that be? What web had caught him in its tenacious grip? Surely there would be another successful treatment to rid his body finally of this horrible disease and lead him to good health. Miracle stories of cancer cures were told every day. Many procedures and chemotherapy treatments followed. Many sleepless nights. Many, many prayers. Many disappointments. All the efforts, this time around, were to no avail. This opponent was far too mean and cunning. Cancer would win. Phil left his wrestling shoes on the mat of life September 7, 2010.

Phil's legacy is continuing with the westling youth groups that he established. Phil's brother, Dave, has renewed the groups with the Phil Nowick Wrestling Club and merged with Mile High Wrestling Club. The club's website at www.milehighwrestlingclub.com gives all the information about getting involved and learning Phil's techniques. Everyone has a lot of fun. —Susan K. Nowick, Phil's mother

PHIL'S EULOGY

SEPTEMBER 8, 2010
FELDMAN MORTUARY

Introduction

My name is David Nowick. I'm the identical twin brother of Phil Nowick ... and I'm not going to say what you think I'm going to say. I have my own spin on life.

My brother Phil wasn't just a good person. He was a great person. You all know that. It's why you are here. I am going to leave most of the historical details of Phil's life and the details of his accomplishments to Rabbi Black. What I'm most concerned about today, and what Phil would be most concerned about, is how you are feeling, what your state of mind is, and how you plan to move forward. So first, I'd like to give you a snapshot of my consciousness and then I'm going to ask you to help me answer a question. I don't want to tell you what to think or how to feel. You pick the answer you like the best.

Snapshot of where I am coming from

My identical twin brother, my best friend, my partner in crime just passed away. That's a fact. I'll bet you are wondering how I am feeling.

Has anyone here ever had a best friend? You had the same interests. You did everything together. You were inseparable. You talked to each other, you called each other, you texted each other every day. Raise your hand if you have had that kind of friend. How long were they your best friend for? How long did that last? How much time did you get to spend with that person? Did you eventually drift apart to find your own path? Did you start a family? Did you get too busy to keep your friendship at that level?

I had my best friend right there for me every hour of every day for forty years. Ask my wife! And I guarantee you, 99 percent of those hours were spent on Broncos football and wrestling talk. On the subject of best friends, I can say that I'll be playing with house money forever. If someone offered you a deal where you would have that kind of friend right by your side for the first half of your life … and then you would have to finish the second half of your life without him, would you take it? I'd take that deal seven days a week and twice on Sunday … actually, twice on Saturday, Rabbi; that's our day because we are Jewish.

Is this a bad day?

Now that you know how I'm feeling, I'd like to get into how you are feeling. Let's start by asking a question. You help me answer. "Is this a bad day?" Those of you who know me know I'm a fairly compulsive person. So, let us try and look at the answer to that question from all the possible angles.

Is this a bad day? Yes.

Let's look at "yes."

On the surface, this seems like an easy answer. You are thinking, "Yeah, Dave, if this isn't a bad day, it sure is shaping up to be a contender."

I've never liked superficial answers, but let's accept yes for now. Let's take a look at what a bad day, even the worst day, looks like in my life.

On a colossally bad day—on the worst day of my life—this is my life:

I have a wonderful wife.

I have two beautiful, healthy kids.

I have great parents.

I have a great extended family.

I have hundreds of my friends here to support me.

I am healthy.

I have plenty to eat.

I am safe.

I live in a nice house.

I live in a wonderful city with a football team that might or might not win this year.

I have the luxury not to have to focus on survival and the privilege to think about spirituality in a time like this. There are people in the world, the majority of them, in fact, whose best day doesn't even hold a candle to the worst day of my life. They live in fear, they live with violence, they live with hunger and disease. Losing a loved one is a normal part of their daily existence.

Gina and I watched a documentary called *Running the Sahara*. It's about two fellows who run across the desert in Africa. I don't remember exactly where in Africa, but they end up in Egypt across from the Red Sea. They were running through the sand dunes and it was very hot. They came across a little boy about seven years old. The little boy was all by himself. His parents had left him to go to get water. It took the parents two days to travel to where they got the water and two days to come back to their son. Can you imagine what that must feel like? Can you imagine those people not having any water? This story sure drove a point home for me.

When you bring gratitude and thankfulness to your life, no matter what happens to you, you feel rich. You feel blessed.

Is this a bad day? Maybe.

Let's look at "maybe."

I'm going to analyze this answer by reading a Taoist parable.

There is a story of an old farmer who had worked his crops for many years. He owned a horse so he was considered rich. One day his horse ran away. Upon hearing the news, his neighbors came to visit. "Such bad luck," they said sympathetically. "Maybe," the farmer replied. The next morning the horse returned, bringing with it three other wild horses. "How wonderful," the neighbors exclaimed. "Maybe," replied the old man. The following day, his son tried to ride one of the untamed horses, was thrown, and broke his leg. The neighbors again came to offer their sympathy on his misfortune. "Maybe," answered the farmer. The day after, military officials came to the village to draft the young men into the army. Seeing that the son's leg was broken, they passed him by. The neighbors congratulated the farmer on how well things had turned out. "Maybe," said the farmer.

I believe in God. I believe our Creator has a plan for me. I just believe we are not wired to understand that plan. When you stop *reacting* to the events in your life—"This is good. This is bad. I should be happy. I should be sad"—then you can start living your life.

Is this a bad day? It doesn't matter.

Let's look at "it doesn't matter."

"It doesn't matter." Life is a cruel series of random events. There is no plan for me. Things just happen to me. That is why a great person like Phil would have to go through something like cancer. This is a dangerous answer, but a very tempting one. Everyone in this room feels like this a little bit. Choosing "it doesn't matter" assumes that we are victims in this life. I would, and I know Phil would, advise you to fight choosing this answer.

I refuse to be a victim. I refuse to be defined by the events that happen in my life. I choose to be defined by my consciousness, by my positive attitude, by the energy I bring to the events in my life. *It does matter.* When you start to live life *proactively,* then you begin to create your own reality.

Is this a bad day? No.

Let's look at "no."

Now that's a powerful answer.

"No" assumes the events in my life, no matter how painful, don't happen *to* me—they happen *for* me

"No" assumes that the events in my life are challenges, meant to bring out the best in me.

"No" assumes that the entire purpose of this crazy existence is to transform—to become more whole, to become something better.

Phil's illness and subsequent passing has been, by far, the biggest challenge of my life. When you see the obstacles in your journey as opportunities, you have a chance to get better as a person. That's when you start winning this game … and I think it is a game.

I have a good friend, Bennie. In the course of a conversation with him about Phil's illness, he talked about an experience with his son. He has a young son who is playing baseball. The age group baseball team was switching from T-ball to coach-pitched. Bennie is kind of a nerdy guy, being a scientist, not the athletic type. Bennie said, "I don't care if he hits the ball or not, I worry about what happens if he strikes out. Will he handle it all right? I don't want him to cry and loose his composure instead of learning from his behavior." I wonder if God sits there and doesn't care if we win or lose but just wonders if we'll handle it in the right way. I believe God is out there rooting for us, just as if we are in a ball game, wanting us to learn from our experiences.

Is this a bad day? It's a trick question.

Let's look at the real answer: "It's a trick question."

A bad day compared to what? Yesterday? Tomorrow? Einstein had a horrible time reconciling the fact that we could remember the past but not remember the future. Neither is real in the physical sense. The past isn't real anymore. The past isn't here. The past forty-eight hours since Phil passed away aren't any more real than twenty-two years ago when he wrestled in the state finals. The future isn't real either. It's this nebulous concept of an unlimited number of possibilities. I'm supposed to compare today to an infinite number of outcomes to decide if it is good or bad?

The real answer

The real answer—and this was Phil's parting message: *today* is the *only day*. Then tomorrow will be the only day. Live it. Live differently. Become something more than you were...but do it *right now*!! If you can do that, then Phil's struggle meant something. It was worth it.

Additional thoughts

Phil made three requests of me before he parted. I'm going to make the same three requests of you.

1. Take care of your body. If you don't have life, you can't be on this Earth.
2. Take care of your family. Stop worrying about yourself and take care of others.

3. Take care of our wrestling club. This, of all of his accomplishments, I think, is the one of which Phil was the most proud. He established Purler Wrestling Rocky Mountain, and it had a really meteoric rise in just a year. I'll continue that coaching group with the Phil Nowick Wrestling Club. The main thing you can do for our family is support Phil's club. You can access the club's website at www.milehighwrestlingclub.com. Root for our kids, come to the practices, support in any way you can. I think that would make Phil happy.

4. **Final Request**

Now I am going to make one final request of you. If you love Phil, I want you to stand up and...CLAP YOUR HANDS!! (Applause for Phil)

— Dave Nowick, Phil's twin brother

THOUGHTS BEFORE TULSA NATIONAL TOURNAMENT

E-MAIL MESSAGE TO MEMBERS OF THE PHIL NOWICK WRESTLING CLUB

COACH DAVE NOWICK

JANUARY 18, 2011

Before a big competition, we are typically focused on what we wish to happen, the possibilities. I have often found it helpful, during these times, to focus on how blessed I already am.

I remember last January vividly. Sometime in between the semifinals and finals of the Tulsa Nationals, I heard my cell phone ring. It was a call from Phil. I was so excited to tell him that our club had two in the finals and a slew of other placers. It was, by far, our best showing ever at Tulsa. And I was sure that he was calling to tell me that he was feeling better and that this "rash" he had been experiencing was resolving.

The tone of the conversation quickly turned. Phil, of course, was happy about our success. He had expected that. However, this was not what he had called to talk about. He had called to tell me that, despite negative blood tests and negative scans for the past six months, his cancer had returned. This time it was in his liver and blocking his bile ducts.

One of the toughest things about being a doctor is that sometimes you have a little too much insight. Stage four colon cancer with distant metastases is an ominous diagnosis. In a millisecond, the implications of Phil's news presented itself in crystal clear fashion. I knew what I was to witness in the coming months. I knew the kind of pain my brother would endure. I knew that, fight as we would, Phil's time on this Earth was short.

I composed myself. I had a job to do: coach our wrestlers to championships and medals in the final round. At that moment, however, I wondered whether this would be that last time I would ever coach. PWA Rocky would certainly not be a reality without Phil. Frankly, I did not see how I could coach without him. I was devastated and truly thought this was the end.

Enter Rick Schultz, who valiantly ran practices using Phil's methods throughout the spring and summer. To our surprise and elation, some thirty kids continued to attend practice and drill... and drill and drill. Enter Tom Clum, Dan Clum, and Todd Legge, who, at Phil's request, so graciously took many of our kids under their wings. Enter the Yapoujian clan, who somehow found a way to reach Phil and get him excited about wrestling, despite the fact that he could not physically step on the mat.

Phil watched the NCAA's and decided we should make a short film breaking down Jason Ness's half nelson to share with Colton, Wyatt, and Lain. Then we made another film, and another. Soon we decided to make a film of the best, most teachable, most drillable techniques from every position in wrestling. We did, and the Phil Nowick System of Wrestling for kids was born. This became the focus of Phil's life. Each day he would pore through film from Flowrestling, technique videos, and live matches on YouTube. Each night I would come home from work, put my son to bed, and head over to my parents' so Phil and I could trudge through "the system." Clip by clip, film by film, we did it. We created a picture of what to teach over time and how to teach it. Many times Phil would have to stand and look at the computer over my shoulder, because it was too painful for him to sit. Oddly enough, we had no venue in mind in which to coach this system. We assumed that I would use it as a high school coach someday... someday.

Near the end of Phil's great life, another idea to form a kids/high school club began to germinate. This time it would be in Phil's honor. It would be his living legacy. Phil did not want the club named after him. It was only after considerable prodding that Jon Yapoujian and I got him to consent to this. Phil had less than a month to live, so time was of the essence.

Enter Vicki Schwartz, who helped me put a club together on the fly. Enter Danielle Hobeika and Lee Walter, who created a logo and website in short order—beautiful images of Phil and his life that would endure forever. Enter Susan Nowick, who put together a collection of short stories Phil had written, compiling them into the soon-to-be-published *Wrestling with Life*. Enter Nick and Estrada, who provided Phil's dream facility in which to coach. Enter the wonderful community of wrestlers and parents that showed up at Premiere MMA Fitness on October 1. They continue to show up.

I never could have dreamed that our program would turn into such a success. Even more exciting, this club is about to grow into something that Colorado has never even seen.

Wrestling is more than a sport. It is hard to explain to someone who isn't involved in wrestling, the way this sport touches your soul and brings out the best in you. It also brings out the best in people around you. Getting back to the original thrust of this e-mail message, in light of the kind of support, the kind of love, the kind of courage, the kind of graciousness that has led up to this endeavor, does it really matter how we place at Tulsa? In competition, I always found that if I could convince myself that I was already blessed beyond my wildest dreams, it took the pressure off. I could relax and wrestle full tilt. Believe me, I *am* blessed beyond my wildest dreams, and I love all of you more than the words of this e-mail can express.

Now relax and go wrestle your butts off! Remember, every match, every takedown, every scramble, every battle for position is sacred. Don't lose even one of them. Remember who and what you represent. It's about the man on the front of our singlets. Nothing else.

— Dave Nowick, Phil's twin brother

POSTSCRIPT

The Phil Nowick Wrestling Club had thirty-five of its seventy members attend the Tulsa National Wrestling Tournament, which was held January 21-22, 2011. This is one of the most well-attended tournaments for age group wrestlers each year. Over 2,600 wrestlers compete, representing forty states. Of course, this large attendance makes the wrestling matches extremely competitive. At the end of the tournament, team trophies are awarded based on the number of placements first through sixth that each team member has won. The Phil Nowick Wrestling Club had the most number of points for its members' placements and was awarded the grand trophy for first place.

Phillip Nowick – 1981 – 1st Place
Little Brother's Cherry Creek Wrestling Tournament

Phil Nowick – 105 lbs - Cherry Creek High School Wrestling Team
Stronghold Wrestling Tournament -
Greeley, Colorado - December, 1986

Dave and Phil Nowick –
Cherry Creek High School Wrestling Team - December, 1987

Phil and Dave Nowick -
Stanford University Wrestling Team - 1991

Phil with Moussee - December, 2001

Coach phil, Thanks for being such a good coach. I won this trophy for you. Love, Danny

Coach Phil Nowick with Danny Trimbach –
1st Place Trophy – 53lbs
Rocky Mountain Monster Match Nationals
Denver, Colorado – October, 2009

Phil Nowick – Spring, 2008

Coach Dave Nowick with members of the *Phil Nowick Wrestling Club*
1st Place Team Trophy
Cliff Keen Tulsa Nationals - January, 2011